International Money Flows and Currency Crises

International Money Flows and Currency Crises

by

István Gyöngyössy

1984 Springer-Science+Business Media, B.V.

Library of Congress Cataloging in Publication Data

Gyöngyössy, István.
International money flows and currency crises.
Translation of: A nemzetközi pénzmozgások és a valutaválság.
Bibliography: p.
1. International finance. 2. Foreign exchange problem. I. Title.
HG3881.G9713 1983 332.4'5 82-24560
ISBN 978-94-017-1949-0 ISBN 978-94-017-1947-6 (eBook)
DOI 10.1007/978-94-017-1947-6

Book information

Joint edition published by: Martinus Nijhoff Publishers, The Hague, The Netherlands and Akadémiai Kiadó, Budapest, Hungary

This is a translation of the revised and expanded version of the original Hungarian book, *A nemzetközi pénzmozgások és a valutaválság*, published by Közgazdasági és Jogi Könyvkiadó, Budapest.
Translated by Katalin Garam and Kornélia Kovács

Contents

INTRODUCTION

The author had already become involved with the subject of this book when President Nixon suspended the convertibility of the dollar on August 15, 1971. This declaration was equivalent to an official admission of the previously evident failure of the international monetary system established in Bretton Woods after long and difficult negotiations. Although the real reasons for this failure are much deeper and more complex, the immediate cause was the tremendous *outflow of money* from the United States to Europe and Japan. Never before had economic history recorded a currency movement of such magnitude, although during the periods preceding the devaluation of the French franc and the revaluation of the Deutsche Mark (i.e., by the end of 1968 and mostly in 1969), and particularly at the beginning of 1971, the international flow of money grew to such huge proportions as to almost traumatize the economic and financial circles of developed capitalist countries. These economic and financial circles correctly foresaw that the ever growing and hardly controllable volume of currency flow could seriously endanger the already precarious balance of the international financial system and perhaps even upset it.

This brief analysis, in contrast to many other predictions of currency developments, holds true for a longer period as well. All the devaluations and revaluations of currencies that have occurred since the period discussed above, as well as the switch of some currencies from a fixed to a floating system of exchange rates (which always denotes a disguised revaluation or devaluation) have been the consequence of large volumes of international money flows.

The direction of previous money flows determined whether the given currencies were later devalued or revalued, or, for formerly fixed currencies, whether the direction of the float was upward or downward.

The continuous and rapid growth in the volume of Eurocurrency markets and the rise of a genuine need for money in the world economy, as well as the general inflation, are contributory factors in increasing the total volume and rate of growth of international money flows, which, however, have become increasingly difficult to register and control. It is therefore understandable that both theoretical and empirical experts in the developed capitalist countries have in recent years increasingly focussed their attention on the problems of international money flows. This increased interest has been inspired by the contemporary importance of such problems, although theoretical economists have been dealing with the causes and laws of international money flows and with their effects on the internal economies of the individual countries since classical times, and empiricists have been interested in such problems ever since the study of international money transactions has formed part of their activities.

The aim of this study is not to settle disputed theoretical problems—though there are many even in the relatively narrow field with which we are concerned—nor to point out previously unknown features, but to *systematize* the phenomena of contemporary international money flows and to make clear their *practical consequences* in the context of the capitalist international monetary system. This work is best classified not in the field of theoretical analyses, but rather among the studies which attempt to disclose the mechanisms of international money flows and the interrelations among monetary phenomena of the recent past.

Perhaps as a result of its empirical character, this study ends on a pessimistic note. In fact, the conclusion of this study is that, given the circumstances, the developed capitalist countries and their central banks cannot influence and limit international money flows to the extent they desire. This statement is thoroughly practical, not only because it is factual, but also because conceptions built upon theoretical bases always naturally lead to a logical solution as they are for the most part *not* based on actual circumstances. In practice, however, especially under capitalist conditions, there are often many factors of a noneconomic nature, which make it difficult or impossible to employ instruments that are recognized as adequate in theory.

*

In order to methodically summarize and expediently survey the nature and operation of the various international money flows, it seemed most appropriate to begin by reviewing the main consequences of the Bretton Woods monetary system and the present situation, and following the definition and structural interpretation of some basic elements, to discuss in detail the Eurocurrency markets on which the most significant money and capital flows take place. Next we shall consider the interrelationships between national money markets and their relation to the Euromarkets; in this section we shall also deal with the effect of international money flows on domestic markets. The subsequent chapter will examine these relationships from the inside, i.e., from the side of the national money markets, with special attention to those powers of issuing currency and granting credit which the central banks can use to influence international money flows. In concluding this chapter we will attempt to synthesize the phenomena introduced and analyzed in the previous chapters. However distinctive or singular, this concluding synthesis—like every synthesis—must be based on principles. Finally, we will endeavour to briefly relate the discussion as a whole to the fundamental aspects of the present international monetary system. This sums up the basic structure of this study.

*

In spite of the author's best intentions, the study is to a certain extent one-sided—or at least not entirely general—in two respects: first, because in this study the author has generally adopted the so-called central-bank view, and, secondly, because most of the material used for this study is of French origin, although this latter bias can perhaps be partly justified by the fact that the French recent past is markedly rich in currency and monetary experiences (e.g., foreign exchange control, the double exchange market, quantitative credit restrictions, and the floating of the franc). Moreover, given the focus of this study, the adoption by the author of the central bank view is not a serious fault and is even justifiable to a certain extent, since national sovereignty—with respect to international money flows—is embodied in the central banks, and it is through the medium of the central banks that these money flows affect the economies of the individual countries.

From a subjective point of view, the central-bank and French-oriented aspects of this study are justified by the fact that the departments of the Banque de France were extremely helpful in the preparation of this study by placing at my disposal material on internal statistics and banking practices. The author owes them a great debt of gratitude. Undoubtedly, the French experience cannot be generalized without qualification, since the French economy and banking system rely more on the state than is the case, for example, in West Germany. This conforms to the French etatist idea, which is both the cause and the result of this situation. The phenomena to be examined (i.e., those accompanying international money flows) demonstrate that *every* capitalist state—however it may try to maintain the pretence of economic liberalism—is compelled in the last resort to use etatist means, to interfere, in order to exert some control over such money flows. This statement, as we shall see later, is true even for those countries whose currency is floating. The question is, rather, whether the instruments at the disposal of the capitalist state are adequate.

*

The author has tried to be accurate in his use of technical terminology and to exercise special care for the correct use and the real meaning of such terms as "money", and "capital", or "currency", and "foreign exchange". This was sometimes difficult and in some places may give the impression of affectedness, since common usage often confuses such terms as "money", "capital", "money flow" and "capital flow", although "money" is a more general word, covering the concept of "money-capital" as well, while the term "capital" usually denotes medium- and long-term money. In Hungarian usage, however, the term "flow of errant capital" is commonly employed, and it would be inappropriate to substitute another term for this expression, even where obviously short-term money flows are being discussed. Similarly, we usually talk about "liberal" or "restrictive" foreign exchange policies, and there is no reason to deviate from such usage when we are discussing restrictiveness and/or liberalism in regard to actual foreign currencies. It is true, of course, that foreign currency embodies the debt of the state issuing it. In addition, common, and even professional Hungarian usage often employs the term "foreign exchange" instead of "foreign currency" or simply "currency", basically in the sense that while currency can be either national or foreign, foreign exchange always means foreign money, either actual money or a claim. Under such circumstances, it would be misleading to employ the term mentioned above too consistently.

Chapter I

The Bretton Woods International Monetary System

In approaching our subject, we must first discuss the capitalist international monetary system itself in the context and through the mechanism of which the extremely rapid growth in the volume of international money flow has occurred. The international monetary system, which was finally wrecked on August 15, 1971, after a long-lasting latent crisis which was the direct consequence of international money flows, was founded in Bretton Woods in the United States at a conference in July 1944, at the end of World War II. Both at the conference and in the subsequent agreements, i.e., those establishing the International Monetary Fund (IMF) and the International Bank for Reconstruction and Development (World Bank), it was predominantly the influence of the United States that prevailed. The economic and political power of the United States was decisive because, in contrast to that of the other countries taking part in the agreements, it had increased as a consequence of World War II.

The IMF and the World Bank, at present with more than 140 members, involve almost all the capitalist countries except Switzerland. The IMF was created in accordance with the UNO Statutes, which means that originally no countries on the losing side of World War II could be accepted as member. Although it participated at the Bretton Woods Conference, the Soviet Union did not join the IMF. Of the socialist countries, Yugoslavia has been a member since the establishment of the organization and Romania joined in 1972. Czechoslovakia and Poland, having been on the winning side, were members originally, but the former, under the pretext of non-fulfilment of her obligations, was excluded, while the latter resigned. In 1964, Cuba left, too. In 1982, Hungary and Poland applied for membership, which was granted to Hungary later in the year but Poland's status is yet undecided. The already unified Viet-Nam, inheriting the membership of South Viet-Nam, as well as Cambodia and Laos, on a continuity basis, have remained members ever since 1976. China was among the founding members, but its rights having been enjoyed by Taiwan in the IMF as in the UNO, and its IMF membership, after lengthy negotiations, was finally recognized in April 1980. This meant, at the same time, the exclusion of Taiwan, until some form of cooperation with the Fund can be found. Switzerland has a unique position, hitherto not wishing to join the IMF on account of neutrality considerations, but—being nevertheless in close cooperation with the organization—it is a *de facto* participant in the international monetary system.

In practice, the Bretton Woods international monetary system was developed within the framework of the International Monetary Fund. The main objective of the international monetary system established at Bretton Woods was to gradually eliminate the constraints on international trade (flow of goods) as well as those on international money flows, and, by gradually lifting the economic restrictions caused by the war, to restore free international trade and money flows. To this aim, the so-called system of "fixed rates" was introduced: the national currencies of the member countries had on official rate (parity), denominated on gold or in one of the designated key currencies and announced to the IMF. Each currency was permitted a 0.75 percent fluctuation vis-à-vis its official fixed rate; if the margin on money markets was greater than 0.75 percent, the central banks were to intervene, buying to prevent a further fall in their currencies, or selling to avert a further rise. For this purpose, the central banks needed reserves either in gold or in foreign (possibly key) currencies. Thus the Bretton Woods pegged exchange rate system was in essence a return to the former "gold-exchange standard".

The gold-exchange standard was first implemented officially by the Genova Conference of 1922, although this was, in fact, only a recognition of the actual situation, since for a long time certain central banks had kept their reserves not only in gold but also partly in pound sterling. These reserves in pound sterling were invested on the London money market. The decision of the Geneva Conference to give up the gold standard and to introduce the gold-exchange standard was motivated by the relative scarcity of official gold, by the difficulty of increasing the quantity of it available, and by the argument that the growing demand for money—a consequence of post World War I reconstruction efforts—would have completely dried up national liquidities had gold continued to serve as the only security. Since its initial establishment, the gold-exchange standard was frequently criticized, and not without reason. Here it is sufficient to mention only the two most fundamental criticisms. The first was that the gold-exchange standard induced inflation, because on the basis of a certain quantity of gold a twofold issue of currency occurred: first one country issued a key currency based on gold, then another country, taking that currency into its reserves, issued money on the basis of it. The other criticism was that the gold-exchange standard allowed those countries whose national currencies were also key currencies to have permanent balance-of-payments deficits, because they did not have to settle such deficits in gold, but could settle them in their own currencies—in paper. This latter situation—which arose within the Bretton Woods monetary system to the particular advantage of the United States—will be dealt with later. It suffices to note here that these two processes explain how, in accordance with the rules of the game in the Bretton Woods system, the balance-of-payments deficit of the US, embodied in excess dollars, enlarged the central bank reserves of other countries.

In order to eventually eliminate the constraints of money movements, the Bretton Woods monetary system stipulated the convertibility of the participating countries' currencies. This convertibility, however, was stipulated only for the currencies among themselves—they were not meant to be convertible with gold. Thereby the dollar, as the *only* currency convertible into gold, became the cornerstone of the system, since the other currencies' indirect convertibility into gold was assured by the dollar's direct convertibility. Simultaneously with the conclusion of the Bretton Woods agreement, the United States assumed the special obligation that the Federal Reserve would convert the dollar claims of the central banks into gold at the official dollar—gold exchange rate. In return, the dollar's official parity was guaranteed by the *other* (foreign) central banks, since they, not the Federal Reserve System, were required to intervene in order to keep the dollar within the permissible limits.

This obligation to intervene, prescribed by the Bretton Woods Agreement, meant that the stability of a given currency—unless, as noted above, it was a key currency—depended primarily on the country's balance of payments. A national currency could be stable on international money markets only if the balance of payments of the issuing country was more or less in equilibrium. More explicitly, if a country experienced a large and persistent deficit in its balance of payments, the supply of its currency on international money markets grew so large that the issuing central bank was forced to intervene and buy back large amounts of its own currency, exhausting its reserves, and thus endangering the stability of its currency. A large and prolonged balance of payments surplus also threatens the stability of a given country's currency. In this case, the international demand for the given currency increased the foreign currency reserves of the issuing central bank. This increase in the reserve base, or more precisely, the consequent increase in domestic currency led to an inflationary boom and a rise in interest rates which in turn endangered the international position of the currency. The restoration of balance-of-payments equilibrium could be achieved most effectively by changing a currency's parity—by devaluation or revaluation. Devaluation makes a country's exports cheaper and its imports more expensive, thereby reducing the balance-of-payments deficit through its effect on the balance of trade. Revaluation, by making exports more expensive and imports cheaper, has the opposite effect on the balance of payments. Moreover, the change in a currency's parity, as we shall see later in greater detail, has a "soothing" effect on money flows, and can change their direction by allowing other factors (e.g., differences in interest rates) to come into play.

In consideration of the close connection between balance-of-payments equilibrium and the parity of a given currency, the Bretton Woods monetary system was designed to allow changes in currency parities. The countries participating in the agreement had the right to change the parity of their currencies by a cumulative ±10 percent upon formal declaration to the IMF, and by even more with IMF approval. On the basis of this aspect of the Bretton Woods system, critics have argued that the system was just as rigid as the gold standard (fixed parities), but ensured stability as little as did interwar monetary practices, which had *de facto* allowed almost unlimited freedom to change currency parities.

At the time this much criticized regulation was framed, chronic balance-of-payments deficits and the devaluations which resulted therefrom were seen as a fundamentally more serious danger. Experiences during the period between the two world wars also seemed to support this view. Even when the IMF started functioning in March 1947, and at the time when commercial demand substantially exceeded supply (due to the lack of goods), a balance-of-payments surplus and the difficulties stemming from it were not considered very serious. In such circumstances a revaluation, which made import prices less burdensome, would have increased export prices also, but in the economic boom caused by the Korean War everything could be sold, even at higher prices. Of course, balance-of-payments deficits and surpluses can only appear together, because the surplus of one country appears as the deficit of another. The time that has passed since the establishment of the IMF has shown that a persistent balance-of-payments surplus can also cause problems.

In any case, it is now clear that the Bretton Woods monetary system and its executive organ, the IMF, could not exert influence on the member countries with respect to the *causes* of parity changes so it would have been useless to forbid such changes. The IMF, because of the strict limitations imposed by its statutes, is similarly ineffective in controlling and restricting international money flows (especially speculative capital flows). In contrast to the ideas of J. M. Keynes, H. White, head of the US delegation at Bretton Woods—as if he had anticipated the appearance of Eurodollars—strove, successfully, to keep the IMF's authority in this particular area as narrow as possible. (This aim, by the way, accorded with the fundamental goals of Bretton Woods: an integrated capital market and the untrammeled functioning of the international money and capital markets.) The reason for the conduct of the United States in this regard was to forestall any actions by the IMF that would endanger the privileged position of the United States in the international monetary system.

As time passed the privileged position of the United States was *de facto* enhanced to such an extent that by the years immediately preceding the announcement of the Nixon regulations in August 1971, the international monetary system had come to be based essentially on a dollar standard instead of on the "gold-exchange standard". This occurred because the dollar had, for all intents and puposes, gradually become inconvertible not only with gold but with the other currencies as well. (The cause of this *de facto* inconvertibility was that the dollar claims of foreign countries had increased to such a degree that the United States would have been unable to cover them with all of its currency and gold reserves if the holders of these claims had presented them all at once, or at least in large amounts.)

How could this situation have arisen? It was the direct result of the political and economic predominance of the United States vis-à-vis the other member states of the IMF, an ascendancy which entirely prevailed within the context of the Bretton Woods monetary system, and whose unrestrained assertion was energetically sought by the United States. The dollar was at once a key (reserve) currency and the "international" currency by means of which—partly for historical reasons and partly due to the enormous economic potential of the United States—the greater part of world trade and money movements was, and still is, accomplished. Since the dollar was a reserve currency, the prolonged and ever increasing deficit in the US balance of payments did not endanger American economic stability for a long time. The contemporaneous utilization of the dollar as the "vehicle" of international turnover led to a state of affairs in which payments in dollars were widely accepted. Moreover, the dollars so acquired were willingly used further with no indication of a desire to convert them—even if the possibility of conversion had existed at that time.

The dollars—which were really just dollar claims on sight against the United States—could end up in one of two places: in the central banks, as increases in the currency part of their reserves, or, either directly or perhaps indirectly through the central banks, on the Eurodollar market. From the very beginning, the United States endeavoured for more than a decade to save its own reserves, and with this end in view, to minimize the presentation to the Federal Reserve of dollar claims for conversion. Hence the United States exerted pressure on the central banks of the more important participating countries by various, often political means to induce them to hold the greater part of their currency reserves in dollars and not to convert them into gold. It is worthwhile in this connection to recall the political criticism provoked in the United States by de Gaulle's position, an attitude which was subsequently embodied in the conversion of most of the dollar reserves of the Banque de France into gold.

In March 1968, the gold pool was dissolved and the convertibility of the dollar into gold became more restricted. This was the first step towards the complete abolition of the dollar's convertibility because from this time onwards the Federal Reserve restricted even the central banks' option to convert their dollar holdings into gold since it limited dollar conversions into gold to only those central banks which promised that the gold they obtained by converting dollars would not be sold on the open market, but used only for inter-bank settlements. This action was supplemented by confidential promises from many of the central banks (the resolutions were taken in the meeting of the Group of Ten) that for the time being they would not seek to convert substantial amounts of dollars into gold. At the same time, the central banks' gold reserves were "stabilized", since those central banks which took part in the agreement were also committed not to increase their gold reserves through direct buying from the gold-producing countries. These measures made the dollar practically inconvertible, and in essence denoted a shift to the dollar standard since the central banks' obligation to buy dollars for intervention was not abolished at that time.

As far as the dollars going to the Euromarkets were concerned, the continuous increase in their number was obviously to the advantage of the United States because (in addition to the versions to which we will shortly turn) no one presented these dollars for conversion, so these dollar sums did not affect the ever decreasing reserves of the Federal Reserve System. Thus, it evolved that the practically inconvertible dollars steadily increased central bank reserves and the volume of dollars on the Eurodollar market.

This situation clearly presented a significant danger, since nobody could control the Eurodollars in the way that the central banks controlled their domestic currencies. The "foreign"—from the American point of view—countries in which these Eurodollars circulated could exert hardly any influence on their markets, since it was a question of dollars and not of their own national currencies. Nor could the Federal Reserve affect them, since these dollars were "Eurodollars", and as such escaped the sphere of the Federal Reserve's stricter control. The rapid, and not infrequently speculative, movements in these masses of virtually uncontrollable Eurodollars were one of the main causes of the crisis in the monetary system. The situation was dangerous and unhealthy also because, as a consequence of the privileged position of the dollar, American economic phenomena affected the whole capitalist economic system, thereby making American domestic inflation universal—in fact, actually "exporting" it through the medium of the dollars circulating ever more abundantly in the veins of the international capitalist economy.

Moreover, after the changes described above and as a direct result of them, the Bretton Woods system was profoundly unfair to all the partners of the United States for the simple reason that American capital could use inconvertible dollars to pay for the very real goods which it purchased abroad. Thus the influx of American capital, the acquisition of foreign companies by American firms, etc., was in fact paid for by advanced capitalist nations—on whose accounts the invasion of American dollars had appeared. Since they kept the dollars received in exchange for American purchases, these countries actually financed the prolonged balance-of-payments deficit of the United States, which arose in part from precisely these purchases. American capital created a complete network of companies abroad. On the total value of the United States' direct foreign investments reached 166 billion dollars, not including reinvestment of profits. These American companies established abroad—80 percent of which were and continue to be the real strongholds of American economic imperialism.

The Bretton Woods monetary system and the United States' perpetual abuse of the opportunities it offered carried within themselves the seeds of their own collapse. The US balance-of-payments deficit continuously increased, the reserves of the Fed—in spite of the restricting regulations—diminished by alarming amounts, confidence in the dollar was justifiably shaken, and, drawn by the differences in interest rates, the outflow of capital began, streaming first into West Germany. Since the United States did not want to restore equilibrium in its balance of payments by devaluing the dollar, not the least for reasons of prestige, it exerted an ever greater political pressure on its important European partners and Japan—i.e., on its most important competitors in trade—to revalue their own currencies, thereby improving the competitiveness of US exports.

This is not the place to review in great detail the financial history of the recent past; we only wish to outline the mechanisms and the consequences of the Bretton Woods monetary system. Therefore, it is sufficient to say that the symptoms mentioned above finally developed to such a degree that on August 15, 1971, President Nixon was compelled to apply measures which signified the end of the Bretton Woods monetary system. These steps, first of all, were that the convertibility of the dollar into gold, as well as into other currencies was completely suspended for an indefinite period of time; the inconvertibility of the dollar now prevailed, not only *de facto* but also *de jure*. In addition, a 10 percent import tax (later abolished) was imposed, which increased import prices just as surely as if the dollar had been devalued by 10 percent. Finally, a three-month freeze on prices, wages and rents was introduced.

The "suspension" of the dollar's convertibility not only upset the bases of the Bretton Woods monetary system in principle, but also brought about serious practical consequences, primarily because this action actually sterilized the central banks' enormously increased dollar reserves while reducing the opportunities of using them. Nevertheless, the central banks were forced to continue buying dollars to intervene on money markets, because if they had not done so, their national currencies would have been exposed to substantial *de facto* revaluation. Therefore, simultaneously with the suspension of the dollar's convertibility, some central banks suspended their own obligations to intervene—(France, for example, introduced a double exchange rate)—and floated their currencies, without, however, being able to avoid intervening in order to maintain their own competitiveness in international trade.

The unilaterally-enacted inconvertibility of the dollar also had a paralyzing effect on the work of the IMF: since the United States had exhausted its drawing rights at the IMF, that organization could not accept payments in dollars. So when a member state, the United Kingdom, wished to meet its dollar obligations to the IMF, it could not do so. The other member states did not want to buy dollars from Britain, which would have enabled that state to settle its debt in other currencies. If, on the other hand, Britain had tried to obtain substitute currencies in the market, this would have caused a further rise in the exchange rate of these currencies, or equivalently, a further fall in the value of the dollar. In spite of these problems the United States was unwilling to effect such exchanges from its own reserves.

It is clear from the examples above that the unilateral steps taken by President Nixon in August—which in fact cancelled the Bretton Woods capitalist monetary system—could not result in a stable and tenable state of affairs. Confidence on the dollar was not restored, and the uncontrollability of money flows led, at ever shorter intervals, to monetary crises. It was obvious that the parities of certain industrial countries' currencies vis-à-vis the dollar and with respect to each other were unrealistic. Other measures were needed. These new arrangements could no longer be unilateral, nor, as it happened, were they developed within the framework of the IMF. Instead, they were achieved on the basis of an agreement of the Group of Ten. The Group of Ten, as a matter of fact, consists of eleven countries: the United States, West Germany, Great Britain, France, Japan, Belgium, The Netherlands, Italy, Sweden, Canada and Switzerland. (The last is the eleventh, as it is not a member of the IMF.) This group is often considered the assembly of the "world's richest capitalist countries".

A compromise (the Smithsonian Agreement) was reached in December 1971. Its fundamental effect was to change the parities of some of the currencies. The US dollar was devalued with respect to gold and the Deutsche Mark and the Japanese yen were revalued. The margins within which currencies were allowed to float were widened from ±1 per cent to ±2.25 percent. The United States abolished the 10 percent import duty it had imposed the previous summer on the assumption that the newly-determined parities now made it unnecessary.

Although the devaluation of the dollar signified beyond a doubt the overthrow of a taboo, it was by no means costless from the standpoint of the other countries concerned. The price of the devaluation was the reassumption by the central banks of the Group of Ten countries of the obligation to defend the new parity of the inconvertible dollar, i.e., to intervene in favour of the dollar. This obligation—in contrast to the Bretton Woods rules—now became formally unilateral, because now the Federal Reserve *de jure* neither converted dollars nor intervened on money markets. This signified the legal introduction of the dollar standard and, as a matter of fact, made the devaluation of the dollar a theoretical fiction, since—as Milton Friedman pointed out—the amount of dollars for which the Federal Reserve will not sell gold does not matter at all.

By the time this compromise—which was supposed to remain in operation until the promised reform of the monetary system—had been reached, it was already obvious that the hybrid situation it created could only have lasted if the balance-of-payments equilibrium of the United States was restored. That, however, did not occur, and the relative tranquillity on international money markets did not last even a month: the price of gold leapt higher, the direction of short-term money flows did not change, and speculation against the dollar continued to such an extent that the central banks were forced to intervene on a massive scale in order to maintain the parity of the now legally inconvertible dollar. Thus it was that in February 1973, barely a year after the first devaluation, the dollar was devalued for the second time. However, it was of an even greater import for the final disintegration of the Bretton Woods monetary system that, simultaneously with the dollar's second devaluation, the central banks of the IMF members revoked their obligations to intervene in the interest of the dollar. With that, the dollar began to float.

This was the beginning of the universal floating which still characterizes the state of affairs among certain currencies, in spite of the attempt—in cases a successful attempt—on the part of some countries to establish a common float of their currencies against the dollar, or to limit the amplitude of the oscillations of their currencies against each other. So in theory, with the above exceptions, currencies now float freely versus the dollar and among themselves; their parities are only nominal. This does not in the least mean, however, that the central banks would not intervene in order to keep their national currencies at the desired exchange rates. They are forced to do so, not only in the interest of foreign trade and for political and economic reasons, but also by the ever larger volume of international money flows, which can be offset only by massive interventions.

The present system of floating exchange rates will most likely last for a long time. Although the IMF conference in Jamaica in January 1976 wanted to lay down some basic principles in connection with the reform of the monetary system, it implicitly postponed the reform indefinitely with its decision to introduce a general exchange rate system "in due course". The appropriate time for the reform will be when general economic stability is restored and consequently an arrangement would be possible which would be equally acceptable to countries with balance-of-payments deficits and to those with balance-of-payments surpluses. The IMF's decision to postpone the reform is equivalent to a sanctioning of the present situation, i.e., the floating.

The efforts of the EEC countries to limit the fluctuations in their currencies at least among themselves were not successful. Britain was compelled to leave the European "currency snake" soon after its birth: a few months later Italy, too, had to float its national currency against the currencies of the other member countries. France, as a consequence of the oil crisis in January 1974, was forced to float the franc (i.e., the commercial franc, as the so-called financial franc was already floating). France's central bank reserves had diminished by 1 billion dollars within a few days, thus, to protect its interests, that country, too, broke away from the "common floating" block of the EEC countries. (In the summer of 1975 France returned to the "snake", but soon had to leave it again.) As a result of EEC efforts for monetary integration, it was only in 1979—by the creation of the EMS—that the free floating of the respective currencies of the member countries against each other was terminated and permissible fluctuation margins were determined.

It was necessary to deal with the historical background of the Bretton Woods system in some detail in order to clarify how deep and manifold was the crisis that stemmed from the flaws inherent in the mechanism of the Bretton Woods international monetary system and from the abuse of the privileged position of the dollar. The successive crises attributable to the factors discussed above were always accompanied by massive money flows of ever growing volume—in fact these money flows were the direct causes of the crises. The actual aim of the present study is to examine the money flows, their causes and consequences. From this standpoint the brief discussion of the Bretton Woods monetary system in the Introduction and the situation that prevailed after its collapse in fact anticipates some of the analysis in the following chapters, since many of the elements mentioned above will be dealt with in much more detail later. It seemed appropriate, nevertheless, to offer a concise general view into which further details can be placed.

The theoretical interrelationships of the issues to be discussed below are clear; their empirical manifestations, however, are by no means as predictable as would be desirable from a scientific point of view. The reason for this may be the many-sidedness of the problems with which we will be concerned, and the psychological factors inextricably entwined with them. Perhaps that was why Gladstone—in whose time currency problems were far from being as complicated as they are today—said that solving monetary problems has driven more people mad than love has.

Chapter II

Central Bank Reserves, Balance of Payments and the External Monetary Position of a Country

Before delving further into the subject of Chapter I, we have to clarify some of the terminology in order to make their use unequivocal. This is all the more necessary, since they are often used in an arbitrary manner in the economic literature. Our definitions are based on IMF publications. Thus, the aim of this chapter is to give an explanation of the concepts (central bank reserves, balance of payments, external monetary position of a country), to outline the interconnections among them and to give a brief review of the technical links through which they are realized in practice. It is all the more indispensable as money flows are reflected in the balance of payments and reserve positions and vice versa.

The role of reserves in the monetary system is of a regulating nature and this is in connection with intervention activities of central banks. Thus, though the existence and volume of reserves are important from other points of view, e.g., a country's creditworthiness—our aim being the study of money flows—we are now mainly interested in this role connected with intervention activities. What does this role involve? If the exchange rate of a certain fluctuation margin in relation to the respective fixed parity, or below the level held desirable by the respective central bank, the central bank will carry out intervention purchases—in the first case obligatorily, while in the second case voluntarily; i.e., it will buy its own currency so as to raise its exchange rate. It is obvious that for the purpose of such purchases it is necessary to have instantly at disposal liquid reserves representing generally acceptable means of payment. Intending to prevent the countermove or the exaggerated rise of her currency's rate, the central bank intervenes by selling her own currency. The countervalue of the sales in foreign currencies will, of course, increase the central bank's reserves.

It is a generally held belief that the reserves' role and importance in interventions are worthy of attention only in case if these reserves are kept by a central bank having at its disposal a convertible currency of fixed parity. This limited interpretation connected with convertibility is, to some extent, right if this term is not applied legally but in the widest sense, i.e., if the respective currency is subject to regular selling and buying in the money markets. Namely, if the respective currency is not convertible at least in this sense, regular interventions are really not justified, even if the central bank intervenes in certain cases for whatever reason.

As regards the limited interpretation connected with fixed parity, this is less justified, though without fixed parity there is no obligatory intervention, but—as it is discussed later in the respective section on floating—floating is generally "dirty", i.e., central banks intervene, for different reasons, without any obligation, too. This will be, however, dealt with thoroughly in connection with the overstocking of reserves.

Finally, in this context and for the sake of historical completeness, mention is to be made of the somewhat different role of the US (FED) reserves in the Bretton Woods system, all the more as their "melting"—as a basic reason—led to numerous subsequent monetary crises. It is known that, as a result of the mechanism of the Bretton Woods international monetary system, the Federal Reserve was never obliged to intervene. Consequently, the US reserves did not serve intervention purposes directly but, in an indirect way, these reserves were also involved in central bank interventions of other countries paricipating in the system. Namely, when these central banks, complying with their intervention obligation, bought dollars and, as long as the system went smoothly, these dollars, or a part of them, were presented for conversion into gold or other currencies at the Federal Reserve System. The US reserves were geared that this conversion obligation on the part of the USA could be duly met. In the present monetary system this became indifferent, partly because the USA unilaterally abandoned its obligation to convert such presented dollars and partly because since "Jamaica" also the counterpart of this conversion obligation ceased to be valid, i.e., after the present transition period will be over and the general stipulations will enter into force, the Federal Reserve System—similarly to any other central bank—will have to intervene.

As mentioned previously, in order to be efficient and to play their intervention role, central bank reserves must be liquid (liquidity means immediate availability without any loss) and are to contain such elements which are accepted generally and without any reservation in the market—intervention being a market operation—and by the central banks, whereto currencies flow through the intermediation of banks.

Since the heyday of Bretton Woods and even since its gradual dissolution essential changes have taken place in the volume and the composition of reserves, which are worth analyzing all the more so as to offer a deeper insight into the complexity of problems inherent in the functions of the monetary system. Primarily gold and convertible currencies were the liquid components (accepted without any reservation) of the central bank reserves when the Bretton Woods system prevailed. Gold and convertible currencies did not play, however, an equal role. Though gold has the advantage of being an essential component of the reserves and, compared to convertible currencies, has less dependence on exogenous government-level decisions, it cannot be used instantly—or properly, directly—for intervention purposes, as in the money market currency confronts another currency and not gold. Thus, before being used for intervention purposes, gold had to be converted into a foreign currency. The foreign currency into which gold reserves were converted by the central bank intending to intervene had to be convertible currency, being only such currency generally accepted without any reservation for intervention purposes.

Consequently, due to its instant usability, central banks necessarily have to hold a definite quantity of convertible currency in their reserves.

As far as the intervention role of gold reserves is concerned, it practically ceased to exist at the time when the gold pool disintegrated and the double gold price was introduced. From that time on, central banks could sell or buy gold only at the official price. Market prices soon surpassed official ones, later exceeding them many times over. Consequently—even if they had not kept themselves, in respect of selling and buying gold, to mutual agreements restricting sale-and-purchase—central banks took care not to sell gold for intervention purposes, since, due to the considerable difference between the market price and the official one, this would have meant significant losses.

The demonetization of gold in Jamaica and its exclusion from the IMF created a new situation also from the point of view of the utilization and of the measurement of the reserves which will be discussed more intensively when analyzing the current situation.

Reverting to the composition of reserves in the Bretton Woods monetary system, the question arises as to which currencies formed its currency part. It is simple to answer that it was mainly the "key currencies", as the French expression "monnaie de réserve", corresponding to the Hungarian translation of "key currency", refers to the reserve role of the respective currency. (There is also a conception according to which "key currency" has a wider meaning than reserve-currency, but even according to this view a key-currency is also a reserve currency.) In the Bretton Woods monetary system the currency portion of central bank reserves was virtually kept only in US dollars. Partly, because the dollar, being the unique currency directly convertible into gold, represented the axis of the whole monetary system. The system was based upon the convertibility of the respective currencies against the dollar, and the mutual convertibility of the other currencies was in fact the result of their convertibility vis-à-vis the dollar. On the other hand, this had practical reasons as well, the dollar being, as the most frequently used tender in international money transactions, the currency always immediately and without restriction applicable for intervention purposes, while the market of other currencies was much more restricted. And when simultaneously with the operational disturbances of the Bretton Woods monetary system, the intention of getting away from the dollar became ever stronger and bigger dollar amounts were flowing to foreign central banks for the purpose of conversion, this again increased the dollar share of central bank reserves, since the respective central banks, hampered in converting dollars channelled to them, could not but further increase their reserves with the latter. This already foreshadowed subsequent similar complications becoming ever more severe.

Already prior to the final collapse of Bretton Woods, SDRs found or could find a place within the elements of central bank reserves.

The Special Drawing Rights was created by the First Amendment of the Fund's Articles of Agreement which became effective on July 28, 1969. Its main point was that the IMF auomatically allocated certain quantities of SDRs as credit to its members (participants), which expressed their interest therein, in proportion to their quotas, which these members (by now all IMF members are participants) could use according to the respective stipulations, primarily but not exclusively to augment their reserves, i.e., as a reserve asset. Thus, in fact, a "money created out of nothing", a fiat money, or at least a reserve asset has been created by an international organization when the thus created, virtually uncovered volume of assets was automatically allocated by the IMF to its members. The credits thus granted have virtually no expiry. Theoretically, every five years the IMF decides whether a new SDR-volume is to be issued and allocated to its members. At the first instance, up to the first five-year period, the IMF resolved to create SDRs amounting to 9.5 billion. Of this amount, in 1970, 3.5 billion, in 1971, 3 billion, and in 1972 also 3 billion was allocated. Since then, only once, in 1978, was the creation of new

SDR amounts decided, with a total of 12 billion, of which an annual 4 billion was allocated between 1979 and 1981, despite the fact that especially the developing countries — for obvious reasons — urge the issue of further amounts.

The question suggests itself: What is one SDR worth? It is known that at the time of its creation the SDR was equal to the gold par-value of one US dollar, prevailing at that time, thus, formally it was pegged to gold. As a result of dollar's depreciation twice, the SDR, with its gold parity unchanged, was detached from the dollar. Since 1974, its value has been set on the basis of a basket of currencies. The composition of the basket was modified twice, as the composition is not determined by the Fund's Articles of Agreement. The basket was frequently criticized exactly on account of its composition and not without reason, partly because of the participating currencies and partly with special attention to their relative weighting. The dollar played the major role in the basket (with a relative weight of 33%) originally, but also many other currencies of lesser importance participated in it, in varying composition and proportion up to the time of the IMF Board Meeting held in 1980, when the original number of component currencies (16) was reduced to 5. These five currencies are the following: US dollar (with a relative weight of 42%), Deutsche mark (19%), French Franc, Japanese yen and English pound sterling (13% each). The value of the SDR is stated and calculated daily on the basis of the exchange rates of the respective currencies according to the above weighting. Though the SDR was assigned by the IMF to play the role of the main reserve asset, the amount of SDR allocated so far has been scarcely sufficient. The allocation of further SDR amounts is, however, a constant objective and precisely in connection with its reserve role (dollar substitution), and, therefore, we shall return to it when analyzing the present situation. Generally, it should be mentioned in respect to the SDR reserves that their role is similar to that of gold insofar as they are not applicable in direct market intervention, but only after their conversion into convertible currencies. Those central banks, however, which have SDRs in their reserves as "holders" are entitled to interest earnings after the respective amount of SDRs. The profitability of the reserves itself deserves attention to which we shall return later.

Central banks often list also the so-called secondary reserves among their publicized reserves. These secondary reserves consist mainly of the unconditional drawing (credit) possibilities of the respective central bank, expressed in some foreign currencies vis-à-vis the IMF and collaterally with other central banks and the BIS. Such are, for example, the swap credit facilities serving the purpose of mutual aid between central banks, which will be dealt with later. Strictly speaking, these are not effective reserves, all the less as they are not actually held by the respective central banks, nevertheless, they are frequently taken into account as such, and not only in the accounts of the central banks (like the Banque de France) but they also figure in the amount of the official reserves as they are immediately available and they may be immediately utilized after having been drawn.

Conditional drawing rights vis-à-vis the IMF are to be considered as tertiary reserves but as a matter of course they cannot be counted with the official reserves. They are available only through the consent of the IMF, and thus are conditional and also uncertain. Credits which may be drawn in convertible currencies within reasonable limits by a certain central bank from another one may also be taken as tertiary reserves.

When showing reserves, central banks calculate in gross, disregarding whether the reserves at their disposal are owned by them, or are borrowed, or just represent unconditional drawing rights. Thus, for example, in case of "net" calculation, the Bank of England's reserves would have been negative for a long time, since it reported officially $2-3.5 billion reserves over 15 years, while its foreign debts, substantially varying in amount during the same period, considerably exceeded this level. This was, however, far from preventing the Bank of England—in case of need—to take intervention steps for the sake of ensuring stable pound sterling rates and, moreover, it was foreign debt which made it possible to keep its reserves at a relatively constant level.

Central bank reserves are, consequently, gross amounts, which serve primarily intervention purposes and have nothing to do with whether the foreign debts of the respective country or central bank exceed its foreign claims. In this approach central bank reserves may be best compared to the cash holdings of enterprises. An enterprise may be in deficit or even insolvent while disposing of considerable cash holdings.

One of the crucial points of the monetary policy of a country is relating to central bank reserves. The first question is what amount of reserves is desirable, or rather would be desirable, and the second one is what be the right proportion among the individual reserve assets. It is justifield to speak in the conditional mood, since, as it will be seen later in more detail, determining the order of magnitude and the composition of reserves does not depend exclusively on the respective country or central bank, neither in the Bretton Woods monetary system nor in the present one, even if within the conditions of floating they had no intervention obligations.

As far as the volume of reserves is concerned, this is influenced primarily by the in- and outflow of foreign currencies. The means by which money flows are intended to be regulated by the governments will be also spelled out in detail later, as well as those aspects of domestic monetary policy, on account of which both the currency flow and, thus, also the volume of reserves are of primordial importance from the point of view of the individual states. Regarding the utilization of reserves for intervention purposes, and in respect to their volumes, it should be mentioned here that if a currency is seriously threatened, or strongly attacked, reserves, as big as they may be, are hardly enough for intervention at an intensive pace, and in order to go through with it, central banks will be, sooner or later, compelled to resort to other solutions (to be dealt with later), such as raising loans. By the way, loans raised or granted may also influence the level of reserves. If a certain country borrows in foreign currency and uses the borrowed amount for the purpose of meeting some of its payment obligations immediately, such operations do not affect reserves. If, however, out of the loan, payment obligations are only fulfilled subsequently, then the respective borrowed amount, until used for payment, will increase reserves. This follows also from the mentioned gross character of the reserves. Credit facilities utilized by the respective countries from the IMF, in the framework of the unconditional drawing possibility, even in case of subsequent utilization, do not affect the level of reserves, since this possibility, itself, represents a reserve asset. If, however, such an IMF allocation is utilized immediately, the reserves of the country will decrease as a result. In the case of credits granted in foreign currency, the reserves of the lender central bank will again diminish, since the lending could take place only to the debit of the reserves. In case of a swap transaction, the level of reserves may be influenced only by the foreign exchange side of the operation.

The maintenance of the required level of reserves is a primary function of central banks. There are theoretical disputes as to what this level should be. Regrettably, these disputes frequently start from suppositions which hardly exist in practice and elements are taken as constant which in fact vary. Consequently, it seems logical that in the case of the floating of a currency, where there is no parity to safeguard, less reserves are needed. This is true enough, even though in the case of floating the volume of intervention did not really decrease.

Anyway, it is true that the economic situation of a country, its balance-of-payments position, its role in the world money market, and its more or less restrictive foreign exchange management do influence the required level of reserves. From our point of view, it is enough to state that too high reserves are not desirable primarily (but not exclusively) because of the counterpart to their increase: the issue of national currency. Nevertheless, certain financial safety considerations such as creditworthiness and prestige reasons do require that they do not decrease too far, either. On the basis of purely theoretical considerations, it is impossible to decide what the optimal size of a country's reserves is, the required level of reserves depending on liquidity needs. This latter again depends on several circumstances. Primarily, we need to consider what the expectable payment obligations of the country are. This is connected, among others, with the volume of imports, with the maturities of both principal and interest payment obligations, etc. Liquidity and reserve needs also depend on the extent to which the foreign exchange management of a country is restrictive. A further factor is how much the domestic currency of a country is involved in international transactions. For the sake of simplicity, however, the required level for reserves is generally defined in relation to annual import volumes. When the Bretton Woods Agreements were still in force, French reserves, for example, were generally on the level of their six-month import volume. When, following the oil price explosion, they nearly fell to half, the Banque de France resorted to borrowing considerable dollar sums.

Almost simultaneously with the suspension of the gold convertibility of the dollar, namely, June 30, 1971, the official central bank reserves of the important industrial countries were as follows:

Country	Official reserves (total)	(US $ billions) Of which: gold at official price of $35/ounce
Belgium	3.2	1.6
France	5.7	3.5
The Netherlands	3.5	1.9
Japan	7.8	0.6
Canada	4.9	0.8
United Kingdom	3.6	1.1
Federal Republic of Germany	16.7	4.0
Italy	6.1	2.9
United States	13.5	10.5

It is not without interest to show these data as they offer a typical picture of reserves at the time of the dissolution of the Bretton Woods monetary system, both in respect to quantity and distribution. The changes that have taken place in both respects shall be looked into later. The quoted figures give rise to interesting conclusions, even at first sight. It is remarkable how different the policies were which the individual countries pursued in respect of the gold tranche of their reserves. The two extremes were Japan and France. The gold tranche of the former was altogether 7.7 percent, that of the latter 60 percent. It can be stated that the gold tranche was the lowest in those countries where American pressure restraining the conversion of dollar reserves into gold—due to political reasons, too—could be made the most effective.

As mentioned already, while maintaining theoretical gold convertibility of the dollar, but for the sake of saving its own gold reserves, the USA endeavoured, in practice, to attain the least possible conversion of the dollar. This endeavour on the USA's part was most definitely opposed by France, the above-mentioned gold tranche of its reserves are concerned, from the beginning they consisted mostly of gold, and having no intervention obligations, reserves with the FED were intended to serve its conversion obligation. This is why—despite all contrary efforts—the gold tranche of the reserves showed a strongly declining trend: its dollar value being $23 billion in 1951, only $17.5 billion in 1961, $13.25 billion in 1966, and $10.5 billion in 1971.

The total collapse of the Bretton Woods system, floating having become general, the Jamaica-decisions and, above all, the subsequent decreasing confidence in the dollar, have basically changed the above-outlined situation. In order to demonstrate the measure of the changes and to monitor the reasons thereof it is necessary to present certain numerical data, even if they are—due to several reasons—hardly comparable with the earlier ones. According to a survey published on the occasion of the Belgrade General Meeting of the IMF in October 1979, the global year-end reserves in billion SDRs of the members (including Switzerland but not Romania) are as follows:

	1970	1975	1978
Global	93.2	193.8	279.4
of which: FRG	13.6	26.5	41.4
Japan	4.8	10.9	25.7
Switzerland	5.1	8.9	16.6
United Kingdom	2.8	4.7	13.1
France	5.0	10.8	10.7
Major oil-producing countries*	5.0	48.3	46.2

* Algeria, Indonesia, Iran, Iraq, Kuwait, Lybia, Nigeria, Oman, Qatar, Saudi Arabia, United Arab Emirates, Venezuela.

As far as the global figures are concerned, they make comparison difficult all the more as the number of the IMF paricipants is increasing, albeit slowly. It could be misleading to compare, prima vista, the 1971 data with the ones in the above table, as the former were expressed in dollars, while the latter in SDRs. Comparison is made fully unrealistic both globally and in respect to the individual countries by the fact that in the mentioned IMF survey the gold tranche of the reserves was valued at the former official gold price* (35 SDR/ounce) while, at the time of writing this paper (1981 spring), the market price of the demonetized gold "fell back" to about $500, as against the even higher former one. To have a clearer understanding of the real situation, we must add that in the above-stated global amount of SDR 279.4 billion, the gold tranche valued at the previous price amounted to SDR 35.6 billion, i.e., the volume of reserves without gold amounted to SDR 243.8 billion at the end of 1971. Out of it, also according to

* This gold price is based on a double supposition according to which the value of the dollar and of the SDR would be equal and the dollar per ounce price unchanged. However, as the gold valuation system of the various member countries is different, the IMF can hardly proceed otherwise.

IMF data, foreign exchange reserves amounted to SDR 220.8 billion. (The difference consists of drawing rights vis-à-vis the IMF and up to the amount of 12.2 billion of SDR itself.) Finally, also in connection with the real value of reserves, it is to be mentioned that as against the increase of value of the gold tranche over the time, the value of the foreign exchange holdings although not to the same extent, but decreased as a result of the general inflationary trends (exchange rate risk).

However difficult it would be to make any comparison due to the above-mentioned factors, nevertheless, some essential conclusions may be drawn, in spite of the fact that the data reflect 1978 end-year positions and the development tendency proved by them, at least in respect to some important countries has suffered, due to the reinforcement of the dollar at the beginning of 1980, a certain—maybe temporary—break. It is true, anyway, that after the collapse of the Bretton Woods system, the volume of reserves augmented significantly on the one hand, and, on the other, the increase of the foreign exchange holdings was especially remarkable which is, at the same time, the main reason for the global increase, too. The gold tranche hardly changed in quantity since 1971 and if so, only very slowly downward (at the end of May 1979 it was 931 million ounces), thus in this context the only question is whether the valuation is right or not. This is, however, not clear in the IMF surveys. For the sake of completeness it is yet to be mentioned that gold reserves of the EMS member countries decreased, too, in volume. They were, however, not calculated at the official—fictive—gold price. Parallel to this, of course, ECU reserves of a growing trend were created in the EMS-participant countries.

As far as the global increase of the SDRs in the central bank reserves in the last decade is concerned (from 1971 to May 1979 from 5.9 billion to 12.2 billion SDR) it needs hardly any explanation as it is the consequence of new SDR allocations that have taken place in the meantime. Further SDR allocations are continuously sought primarily by developing countries. The ECU is also an artificial reserve asset, which, however, is different in nature from the SDR, first of all because the ECU has a collateral: the part of the EMS participants' reserves centralized with the FECOM.

Reverting to the increase of the foreign exchange tranche of the reserves as the most important phenomenon of the reserves and examining it more thoroughly it can be stated that its global and average rate between 1951 and 1969 was 5 percent. This rate was gradually rising since 1973 (up to 1979) reaching by now about 15 percent per annum. As floating became general in 1973, the increase of foreign exchange holdings is generally believed to be co-related with it. According to other opinions, logically right ones, the floating, disclosing the intervention obligation, has an influence just opposite to the increase of reserves. This is true, but, as we experienced, central banks intervene even without obligation, and to a rather large extent. Consequently, floating itself is neither a reason for the increase of reserves, nor is it enough to keep it down, if, after and despite the intervention obligation has ceased, the necessity and the frequency of the intervention continue to prevail.

Intervention, by way of selling the domestic currency, increases, while through buying it decreases foreign exchange holdings. If these two ways of intervention were virtually on balance, as actually they should be as a consequence of the frequent countermoves of the exchange rates caused by clean floating, this would not lead to essential changes in the level of the foreign exchange reserves. Thus it is obvious that the large and rapid increase of the foreign exchange holdings is attributable to the fact that in the wake of the mostly speculative money flows, central banks and especially some of them were compelled to intervene by way of massive domestic currency sales, i.e., external currency purchases. And this is the main reason for the global increase of the foreign exchange holdings even if such an increase in the case of the oil-producing countries may be considered—being connected with oil-price rises—as inherent in their balance of trade and balance of payments position, but in any way may not be related to the major problems of the international monetary system.

Why were the central banks compelled to intervene with such massive currency purchases? The reason is linked with the dollar—the leading currency of the international monetary system—and its roots go back far into the past. That is why, even at the risk of repeating ourselves, it is worth reexamining the phenomenon. The outflow of the dollar started already at the peak of Bretton Woods, on the basis of the virtually unique key currency, the dollar, according to which the USA could finance its balance-of-payments deficit with its own currency issued in any required amount. The USA did avail itself of this privilege, and even abused it. With its dollars, which, due to their key currency role, were considered equal in value with gold, the USA bought up entire "firm-empires", financed wars, and subsidized certain countries for political reasons. This abuse undermined the sometime general confidence in the dollar which finally led to two subsequent devaluations of the dollar, to the collapse of the Bretton Woods monetary system, to general floating and practically, in a paradox way, to the existence of the dollar standard, in spite of the fact that the dollar issued in ever larger volumes became inconvertible against gold and its convertibility vis-à-vis other currencies is also based on a practical consensus, given that if the dollar volumes held in countries would be presented at once, or at least massively for conversion to the FED, such conversions could not be fully met.

After 1973, confidence in the dollar was reestablished but only for a short period. After about two years, growing amounts of dollar moved out again. These money flows, which increased in volume at the time of the dollar crisis, were new signs but at the same time also causes of the decreasing confidence in the dollar. Weak periods of the dollar were regularly followed by a certain stabilization, but generally at a lower level of the dollar exchange rate than before the crisis. Just because of this abruptness and as in mid-crisis periods the FED generally endeavours to reinforce the dollar with interest regulations; money flows were not unilateral, but tended, however, definitely outward and their average annual volume increased accordingly.

Dollars are flowing in two directions: either as effective dollars to the so-called Euromarket, where they participate in the credit turnover, or—and this is what mainly pertains to our subject as it relates to the lack of confidence in the key currency—they are converted, thus actually contributing to the increase of central bank reserves. International money movements being essentially caused by the assumed exchange rate deviations between two currencies, it is obvious that dollar amounts were converted mainly into currencies the exchange rates of which were judged by the international money circles as stable and of an appreciating tendency vis-à-vis the weak dollar, and this increased the foreign exchange reserves of the central banks holding such currencies. (Foreign exchange reserves of the oil-producing countries do not stem from money flows but from dollar payments for oil purchases.) It is not by chance that in the table showing the global position of reserves, data relating to the various industrial countries figure separately. Due to the aforementioned reason, dollar outflows were directed to these countries and primarily to the Federal Republic of Germany, Japan and Switzerland, their domestic currency being judged especially stable and therefore these countries hold the highest reserves. It is characteristic that foreign exchange holdings of the FRG, having nearly doubled from June 1971 up to December 1979, amounted to $47.25 billion at the end of 1979. The Bundesbank not only had to intervene in favour of the dollar by way of buying up incoming dollars so that the exchange rate proportion between the dollar and the Deutsche Mark did not slip too much in favour of the DM (endangering also the exports), but it has to do so also obligatory, in accordance with EMS regulations in favour of the member countries' currencies, i.e., it had to buy them, too, and had to augment its reserves also for this reason.

It was repeatedly stated that foreign exchange purchases involve issuing domestic currency, which generates inflation if it is excessive. Increase in foreign exchange holdings thus is something like a "thermometer" of this imported form of inflation. It is quite understandable that countries receiving money for conversion try to protect themselves against it. By what means and with what results will be discussed later. First, we wish to see what the respective central banks do with accumulated foreign exchange holdings. They endeavour to profitably mobilize them. While gold reserves are generally held idly in central bank safes, foreign exchange holdings are mostly placed out, their amount being so high that their full utilization for disponibility purposes could, in normal circumstances, hardly take place. Otherwise, central banks intend to counterbalance the so-called exchange rate risk (to be discussed later) by placing a considerable part of their foreign exchange holdings against interest. How do they do it? The most simple way is to place such holdings for short term in the Euromarket. This possibility is, however, restricted by agreements renewed from time to time between central banks with the aim of preventing excessive increase of foreign exchange placings in the Euromarket which may result in inflation and growing speculation. It is possible that these restrictions are sometimes not firm enough or not every central bank respects them. (According to Mr. Lantos and Mrs. Lőrincz, in 1975 around 60 percent of the monetary dollar holdings was placed in the Euromarket.) In any case, the fact is that since several years central banks of the industrial countries have been drawing a profit from the overwhelming part of their dollar holdings in a way that they buy short-term US Treasury bills which, in case of need, may be mobilized in the US stock exchanges.

Nevertheless, circumstances may arise when such profit making becomes contradictory to the basic requirement according to which reserves should be liquid. Namely, liquidity means that a certain asset should be immediately, but also without any loss, ready for mobilization. This liquidity requirement is not at all unconditionally ensured by the selling of Treasury bills on stock exchanges, as such sales may even incur losses, especially when the central bank is compelled to place at once a substantial amount of Treasury bills on the market, which naturally lowers their price. These considerations are, otherwise, far from being theoretical, which they seem to be at first sight. Due, among others, to the dollar's restabilization in early spring 1980, as well as to its own unfavourable balance-of-payments position, the Federal Republic of Germany wanted to mobilize a part of its dollars kept in US Treasury bills. This aroused not only an opposition on the part of the USA, but also the above indicated dangers.

Mention has been made above of the exchange rate risk which means that a currency held by a central bank as reserve asset suffers value losses, i.e., its exchange rate considerably declines. Obviously, central banks wish to protect themselves against such risks by diversifying their reserve assets. Between 70 and 80 percent of the foreign exchange holdings of central banks consists of dollars. Why the dollar share is so high was already explained in the part describing the necessary preconditions for a currency for playing the role of a reserve asset, and enumerating the reasons leading to the unduly high, distorted increase of the dollar tranche in reserves. Diversification of the dollar reserves is not an easy task. It is objectively not the case as no other currency applicable as reserve asset is available in the required quantity. Nevertheless, about 6-10 percent of central bank foreign exchange reserves is in Deutsche Marks. Nor is diversification easy from the technical aspect; with large volumes of currencies being involved in the transaction, the very transaction itself may cause a considerable exchange rate decrease of the currency sold, and an increase of the currency bought which is undesirable from the point of view of the stability and external economic equilibrium of the respective country. Otherwise, diversification in the given circumstances in practice means dollar sales, which, due to their exchange rate implications, also hurt the interests of the USA.

Accordingly, the endeavour of central banks for transforming different reserve elements have rather narrow margins and problems due to the dominant dollar share in reserves (primarily the exchange rate risk) are still unsolved. A return to the gold standard, as a possible solution—given the reasons outlined afore—is not really an alternative. Thus, obviously, interest is focussed on the logically possible third solution, i.e., on the creation of an artificial reserve asset, which could serve at least partly for the substitution of foreign exchange holdings. It goes without saying that this role could only be played by a reserve asset created by the IMF on an international level and naturally the already existing SDR seemed applicable for this purpose—as originally intended. These considerations led to the plan of the dollar substitution account to be established by the IMF. (Officially it was called "substitution" account, but the public interpretation talking about a dollar substitution account was well justified.)

As of the start of 1976, the IMF dealt more intensively with the issue of the decrease of dollar reserves and at the same time with their partial consolidation. Consolidation was also dealt with because the dollar amounts forming a part of the central bank reserves represent on sight payment obligations of the USA; thus if this debt is, in some way, transformed into a long-term one, it means the consolidation of a debt position. The IMF's endeavours were aimed at such a consolidation in fostering that central banks transmit a certain tranche of their US dollar holdings to the IMF, which, in return for the US dollar amounts received and in proportion to their value would have submitted from a dollar substitution account its own bonds denominated in SDRs to the respective central banks. The IMF would have invested such US dollar amounts in long-term US government securities, interest earnings on which would have gone to the central banks placing the dollars.

This conception undoubtedly had more advantages. The major target, the decrease of the dollar share in central bank reserves, would have been achieved and thus for the central banks, sharing this endeavour, this should have been desirable. Simultaneously, it was in agreement with the diversification targets of the central banks, as SDRs, to be received for their dollars, are by definition diversified, being in fact a basket of currencies, even if in this basket the dollar has a decisive role. From the diversification point of view this solution seemed feasible also for the reason that—contrary to the method applied hitherto—it hurt neither the interests nor the prestige of the USA. Finally, such appreciation of the reserve asset role of the SDR might have contributed also to a calmer atmosphere required for monetary stability.

In spite of the overall expectations, however—in the absence of the necessary majority of votes—the General Meeting of the IMF held in Belgrade in autumn 1979 did not bring any resolution to the establishment of the dollar substitution account and regarding the plans connected with it. This was only partly due to the behaviour of the developing countries which, in line with their previous standpoint required that eventual new SDR allocations (and virtually this was the case, though only in exchange for dollars) be effected on condition that a specified portion of the SDR allocations be automatically due to the developing countries needing it. However, it might have been a more decisive factor in this connection that even the most interested countries—the USA and the developed industrial countries—could not agree on certain essential details and thus the final decision was postponed.

Nor was there any progress in respect of the dollar substitution account at the meeting of the IMF Interim Committee held in April 1980 in Hamburg and, apparently, it has been dropped from the agenda for the time being. The causes behind this are worth noting, as, on the one hand, they offer a deeper insight into IMF power relations and, on the other, they clear up the difficulties which are unavoidably met by the IMF even in respect of the partial reform of the international monetary system. As mentioned before, the developing countries posited certain claims against a part of the new SDR allocations. The advanced industrial countries were not willing to meet such requirements through the establishment of the substitution account. The USA gave much less support to this idea than earlier, partly because the necessary approval of Congress was doubtful, but mainly due to the fact that the significant strengthening of the dollar which had started in the meantime, undercut the timeliness of the substitution account from the point of view of both the USA and of the countries with central bank holdings with a substantial dollar share.

The Federal Republic of Germany, which, as we have seen, was compelled to accumulate especially high dollar reserves, has also changed its standpoint regarding the substitution account. Originally it supported this conception, expecting a possible diminution of the exchange rate risk (though this point has lost momentum due to the rise of the dollar's exchange rate), and because it did not want the DM to gradually become a reserve asset. The FRG rightly supposed that the establishment of the substitution account would lessen the pressure for that. In the meantime the country's balance of payments became passive and, according to experts, it will continue to show a deficit not the least because of the oil price rises, which, of course, lessened the opposition to the reserve asset role of the DM seeing that the FRG raises rather large loans from OPEC countries in the form of DM denominated bonds.

All that has been outlined so far only shows that reserve problems, the solution of which was the major objective and task of the international monetary system following the collapse of the Bretton Woods system—similarly to many other problems—have not come any closer to a satisfactory settlement. It is true that the dollar's significant interim reinforcement slowed the dollar flow to the central banks and that certain diversification of reserves took place even without the substitution account, not lastly due to the fact that the FRG's balance of payments became passive and thus the DM received gradually a reserve asset role. This, however, does not solve the reserve problem, on the contrary, it may deepen it. This is due partly to the fact that price fluctuations of reserve currencies are not so much influenced by the purchasing power and the trade balance as rather by purely financial factors, mainly by the differentials in interest levels. Thus, besides the dollar, other currencies becoming reserve assets, like the DM and perhaps also the yen, are increasingly subject to such influences and consequently it may occur that the cohesion of the international monetary system will be the result of the hardly controllable exchange rate fluctuation of two or three unstable reserve currencies instead of one. Furthermore, it does not seem to solve the reserve problem either because all IMF concepts, the substitution account included, were designed to remedy the status quo only, but they never tackled the future development of the level and composition of reserves while nothing seems to assure the avoidance of newly emerging dollar (or eventually DM) surpluses within the reserves.

*

In principle, the balance of payments means the confrontation of the net changes in the liabilities and assets of a country vis-à-vis other countries. Considering, however, that the method of stating the balance, as will be seen later, is, to some extent always arbitrary being a matter of decision as to what elements are combined in it, it seems necessary to reckon with such an element as the external monetary position. This means, in fact, the *real* net position of the respective country's foreign claims and obligations, i.e., of its overall and actual balance of payments. Thus, even if the term "balance of payments" is used later on, it will always cover the more exact external monetary position which equals the actual net balance.

Central bank reserves represent one of the essential elements of this balance as they duly figure on the assets side of the balance of payments. This is the co-relation between the reserves, the balance of payments and the external financial position. Consequently, it is indifferent from the point of view of the external financial position as a net balance whether the central bank uses borrowed currencies or its own reserves for intervention purchases of its own currency. If it intervenes by means of borrowed money, it increases its foreign liabilities, but if it acts by using its own reserves this reduces its assets.

The above definition of the external monetary position is right only if the time factor is included, too. The terminology used in most foreign languages makes differentiating between assets and liabilities of monetary and financial character easy. The external monetary position of a country generally means the net balance of monetary assets and liabilities and we are going to use this expression in the following analysis also in this sense. Logically, since external finances change in function of the time factor and it is conceivable only if specified for an actual date or a brief period. A payment obligation or a claim becoming due, say, within ten years, does not affect the current external monetary position of a country but a next day maturity does, even if sometimes the loan becoming due currently was granted for ten years.

External monetary position has a very similar meaning to that of solvency at the enterprise level. The external monetary position of a country stems from its balance-of-payments position and it is on this basis that the individual countries—though applying different methods—state their actual external monetary position. Indeed, what does external monetary position mean? It means that at a given time or period how and to what extent is a country able to meet its due foreign payment obligations by way of using its foreign claims effective in the same period. Thus, the external monetary position involves both state and individual external claims and obligations of a country, denominated either in domestic or foreign currencies. Changes in the differential balances resulting from totalling and confronting these items show what is important from the point of view of the smooth functioning of the monetary system, i.e., whether the respective country is able to meet its foreign obligations from the claims it has (including central bank reserves). Accordingly, the US external monetary position may be considered negative given that its foreign monetary claims are insufficient by far to meet its external payment obligations. It might be worth mentioning that the term "foreign exchange position" is also frequently used in this context, especially in our country, since Hungary's external trade and monetary relations are not transacted in forints and thus we speak of the foreign exchange position of the country, or about its position in terms of Western currencies, rather than of its external monetary position. The foreign exchange position covers, however, only the balance of the claims and obligation in foreign currencies, and therefore external monetary position has a wider sense.

It might be clear from the foregoing that the external monetary situation at any time may be derived from the balance of payments in a way that the real balance is stated at a definite time or for a short period. Nevertheless, each country states its external monetary position in a different way and the difference virtually depends on which items are taken into consideration and in what way. It was mentioned before that medium- and long-term maturities cannot be reckoned with when determining a country's external monetary position.

There are, however, medium- and long-term claims and obligations which may become immediately due at any time. It was said in connection with reserves that central banks, having overaccumulated dollar amounts, buy US government securities. These securities, representing medium-term obligations of the USA do not affect the external finances of the latter, though they may be sold at any time and thus, upon request of their owner, may be changed into call money.

The same may occur also, but the other way round, when residents keep foreign securities in their portfolio, which is rather frequent. This is a typically long-term investment, or outstanding claim, and for this reason it does not influence the external monetary position, though the owner of such papers may, at any time, sell them abroad, which, obviously, affects the external monetary position of its country. Consequently, it is not always easy to make a definite distinction among various credit and debit maturities.

At one time it used to be fashionable to speak about a basic balance. Visibles and invisibles of the trade balance figured in it, as well as long-term capital movements being due in the subject period, but short-term money movements were, however, disregarded as being of a speculative character, while the balance of payments is designed to register regular and structural money movements. Monetary crises occurring with growing frequency later justified the primary importance of short-term money movements, and therefore new methods started to be applied.

Some years ago, the USA tried to set up its balance "on a liquidity basis". This method took into consideration, besides basic balance items, the short-term US money export as expenditure while the short-term money import—interpreted as liquid liability—was disregarded. This really asymmetric handling of elements meriting equal regard proves how arbitrary viewpoints may dominate balance of payments accounting methods. Since recognizing the disadvantages of the above method, the calculation "on official reserve translations basis" has been applied, which registers short-term capital movements within the banking system, but consequently disregards the short-term claims of non-resident individuals and enterprises towards the USA on the basis of the interpretation according to which these claims derive from dollar-minded decisions of the owners, i.e., this is in fact a money flow to the USA which cannot figure on the liability side of the balance of payments. Such an explanation is hardly justified, the relevant volume itself is not insignificant either. Let us cite just one example to demonstrate what considerable deviations are caused by the application of different methods. In 1966, a relatively calm year from a monetary viewpoint, the US balance of payments deficit "on a liquidity basis" amounted to US $1.4 billion, while "on official reserve transactions basis" the balance was active to the amount of US $0.3 billion.

Theoretically, the external monetary position may be equal with the net balance of payments, practically, however, this may never occur, partly because the balance-of-payments considerations of the various countries are different, partly as none of the balance of payments techniques could encounter all external monetary claims and obligations, not even if—contrary to the above cited

US examples—this really was intended. There is also a view according to which this is definitely not the aim of the balance of payments, but rather the registration of external economic (commercial and financial) transactions even if there is no payment at all, or it takes place prior to or after the transaction. The IMF itself recommends to members the "on official reserve transactions basis" model of balance of payments. These kinds of balances are not applicable to demonstrate the external monetary position or, if so, only by the combination of numerous further elements.

In fact, a similar economic approach is reflected in the so-called "current account" *(Leistungsbilanz)*, too, which encounters the visible and invisible items of the trade balance, wages paid to foreigners, military expenditures, and both interest revenues and payments from and to abroad. Short- and medium-term maturities being, however, disregarded, it fails to provide information on external monetary positions.

The other type of payment balances intentionally aims at registering those monetary movements which take place effectively as a result of external transactions. This sort of balance may be virtually compared to the cashbook. At the end of a certain period, revenues and expenditures are added item by item, and the final balance should equal the positive or negative change in the cash stock. (The role of cash stocks is represented by central bank reserves; they do not figure in the balance of playments, but only their changes.) Balance of payments of this kind are much more applicable for picturing the external monetary position. Several countries prepare both types of balances.

All these details were presented so as to show the different methods and numerous practical difficulties, as well as the resulting inexactitude, too, of drawing up the real and detailed balance of payments, of stating the effective external monetary position. It has been said that setting up the balance of payments is to some extent arbitrary. Supposing that all countries would draw up their balance of payments according to equal guidelines, then principally the aggregated balances should be in equilibrium since the surpluses of countries with an active balance should be globally equal with the deficits of countries with a passive balance. However, in practice this could not occur, not even under equal principles, as gold-producing countries handle gold as a commodity and thus, if it is exported, exports are not shown as a change in central bank reserves, but central banks, which buy it, on the other hand, do show it. This follows, however, from the double role of gold.

It seems worthwhile having a look at the relationship between trade and payments balances. It is well known that trade balance development is an essential factor in the balance of payments position. It is true that the balance of payments in its classical sense does not contain the countervalue of exports and imports, and only the effective money out- and inflows connected with them are taken into consideration. Nevertheless, practical balance-of-payments methods generally take into account the trade balance unchanged, because if the trade balance shows substantial change in some direction, it would cause a parallel change in the balance of payments, too, unless they are offset by other balance of payments items. The higher and the more sudden the trade balance modification is, the less is it possible to offset it immediately by other balance of payments factors. The tripling of oil prices at the end of 1973 is a good example. The price rise of this important fuel caused a deficit in the trade and payments balances of almost all Western European countries.

From the point of view of monetary stability, which economists often appear to forget about, balance-of-payments fluctuations not deriving from the trade balance, i.e., from the trade turnover, but in the sudden, one might say, speculative money-flows, are also of primary importance. They are not shown in the current account which is broader than the trade balance but in the so-called capital account. (Current account and capital account together form the balance of payments.) The expression of capital account may give rise to a misunderstanding in the concrete case, as it contains not only long-term capital movements but also short-term money flows (hot money) and this latter is what is interesting from our point of view. The significant impact of the speculative money flows may be attributed partly to their volume ($100 million a day is not unusual during monetary crises) and partly to their sudden appearance. In fact, larger volumes flow only between countries having a dominant role in the international monetary system and economy but primarily due to this elevated role of the respective countries, speculative money movements have a destabilizing effect of a universal nature.

Capital flows have, besides, also a direct impact on the trade balance. Namely, larger capital inflows, as we shall see later, cause an exchange rate rise in the recipient country. In case of higher exchange rates imports become cheaper and exports more expensive which hurts the trade balance at two sides: exports decrease and cheaper imports increase. This thesis is valid also conversely; capital outflows reduce the exchange rate which makes exports cheaper, imports more expensive—affecting also their volumes.

In respect of trade and payment balance interferences it is yet to be mentioned that capital export generally decreases or at least may decrease commercial exports. This is obvious since goods produced in the framework of external industrial investments realized by means of capital exports will not increase the export volume of the country which invested the capital. External investment projects are generally realized in such sectors of the industry which are well-advanced in the investor country and produced intensively for direct exports, which form will, however, be less in demand at least in the capital-importing country where the respective investment was realized. Thus, e.g., US investments, discussed in connection with the abuse of the key-currency role of the dollar, influenced negatively the US balance of payments in two aspects: partly on account of the capital export and partly due to the slackening of direct commercial exports. The deterioration caused by these two factors may be only partly offset by the repatriation of profits resulting from the mentioned investments.

Reverting to the various balance of payments methods, it is clear that their application may be justified because of economic considerations, of their relatively simple feasibility, they may, nevertheless serve the right presentation of the external monetary position only if all elements present at the given time or period have been taken into consideration, even in such case, however, the respective elements may be calculed differently, as amply proven by the above-cited examples.

The external money and credit relations of a country involve quite a number of transactions which affect neither the central bank reserves nor the external monetary position because these transactions often compensate each other and they are realized only within a certain lapse of time, or when their manifestation later reaches a stage when they are already influencing reserves and the external monetary position.

The most typical case of the delayed influence is the sale on credit against foreign currencies. The resulting claims will affect the external financial position only when credit maturity approaches but do not necessarily hit central bank reserves even if the debtor has already paid. If payment took place by cheque which is not cashed for a certain period by the creditor or it is cashed at an external bank, as well as in the case when the debtor pays in favour of the creditor to an external bank, the amount of reserves remains unchanged, and will change only when the due amounts are repatriated by the creditor. Even this having happened, the impact on reserves is still not certain, it will become effective when the creditor converts the foreign currency into his domestic currency (if there is no conversion, reserves are not concerned) and this in the money market, i.e., selling takes place through the banking system, since this way the relevant currency amount will finally reach the central bank in return for the domestic currency. The same transaction will not affect central bank reserves if the resident creditor sells its currency not in the market but straight to the importer or to an individual who uses it for external payment or accumulates it, in other words, the currency does not reach the central bank through the banking system. In connection with central bank reserves, the rule may be stated as follows: all market sales of currency increase them, while all market purchases decrease them.

The case referred to in the previous paragraph—namely, that the resident seller itself or the bank which got the respective currency amount does not convert it with the central bank but accumulates it or uses it for some other purposes—is rather frequent. Consequently, a certain stock is formed in the currency of the buyer's country which—from the point of view of the buyer's country—represents in fact sight external debts, thus affecting the external monetary position, but central bank reserves of the buyer's country are not influenced by external purchases for domestic currency, or one may say that such purchases save the reserves, central bank reserves will decrease only if the foreign seller or the one receiving the countervalue converts it into its own currency.

The thus created currency stocks—Eurocurrencies—which may be quite substantial in the case of hard currencies or, especially in the case of key currencies, though advantageous for the issuer countries by temporarily saving their central bank reserves, they may, nevertheless, also become dangerous from the point of view of the monetary stability of the respective country because if all the holders required at once their conversion with the intermediary of their central banks, this of course would finally seriously affect the issuer country's central bank reserves. This is why the issuer countries try, if possible, to avoid the run of excessive conversion requirements on their central banks (USA), or they endeavour to ensure external help in advance, should such a case occur (England, sterling balances).

Concerning reserves, the external monetary position and their interrelations, it can be also stated that there are several transactions affecting the money and credit relations of a certain country which concern only central bank reserves without influencing the external monetary position of the country. This happens in all cases when an importer—buying from abroad with foreign currencies but unwilling to undertake the exchange rate risk—covers itself either in cash, immediately buying the currency needed for the payment of the countervalue from its bank or a forward base where the bank undertakes the obligation to sell him the necessary currency amount at a rate and for a time fixed in advance. In the latter case, the bank generally acquires from the central bank the amount of currency necessary for the fulfilment of its obligation, i.e., the bank covers itself, too. Anyway, there is an advance currency purchase, decreasing the currency stock of the central bank, thus its reserves. The purchased currency will, however, remain for a time with the central bank or with the importer, consequently the external monetary position of the country does not change, but only certain modifications occur within its components since the currency amount in question went elsewhere from the central bank, i.e., to the banking sector.

If instead of an advance currency purchase there is a case of selling it in advance, which happens, e.g., when an exporter sells on a forward base for domestic currency the foreign exchange countervalue, i.e., before cashing it, then the external monetary position of the country does not change either and there is only a shift in the opposite direction between the central bank and the private economic sector.

In the examples mentioned so far time was the major influencing factor. More frequent and, above all, more important are those operations which, while compensating each other, remain in one or in another respect ineffective. The most significant are the so-called swap operations, which, although they are affecting central bank reserves, have no influence on the balance of the external monetary assets and liabilities of the country, in our own terms, on the external monetary position. Swap is an operation of two partners from different countries, who grant loans to each other mutually in the same value and for a definite, equal period and in their respective domestic currencies. The significance of swap operations is precisely the fact that when a central bank meets difficulties due to insufficient reserves, another central bank renders assistance in this form. These operations substantially helped some important central banks to get through certain critical periods and to avoid, at least temporarily, the devaluation of their currency, as their reserves having been increased by the amount of the swap, intervention purchases could be pursued. The central bank assisted with the swap uses the received foreign exchange, while the central bank giving the assistance keeps it in some way. The external monetary position of the respective countries, however, did not change, because against the credit received in foreign exchange claim was created in an equal value in domestic currency or vice versa.

The other form of assistance between central banks is when a central bank places a deposit with the other one in its own currency (or from the point of view of the bank to be helped, in foreign currency). In our view this is the same case as the previous one: the reserves of the deposit taking central bank grow (besides this being the aim of the whole operation), but the external monetary position of the country (moreover, its foreign exchange position) does not change either, because though its foreign exchange stocks grow, given that the deposits are being encountered as short-term debts, its foreign exchange liabilities increase simultaneously. The situation is the same with the swap operations, as swaps—similarly to deposits—even if they may be renewed, are in principle valid only for short terms. It should be mentioned that swap assistance is more frequent than the one through deposits due to the simple reason that the central bank statutes of most of the advanced Western countries do not allow the respective central bank to place deposits, i.e., unilaterally grant a loan to an other central bank. Swap operations were brought to life to circumvent this rule.

Swap lendings as a form of mutual aid between central banks were first massively used in March 1961 when central banks regularly participating in the Basel Talks granted a $1 billion swap opportunity to the Bank of England. In 1962, Canada and then Italy availed themselves of larger swap amounts and in the same year the Federal Reserve System, too, started to build its swap network. By the end of 1962, the USA had swap contracts to an amount of $900 million which, by the end of 1968, grew to $10.5 billion and by the end of 1977 to $20 billion. The network of bilateral swap contracts include the central banks of all advanced Western countries. These bilateral contracts ensure for the partner mutual swap possibilities in amounts generally fixed in advance. A telephone call is enough in such cases to make the necessary drawing, therefore the swap is easily applicable. In dangerous monetary situations central banks prefer to have recourse to this means which is why crises and massive swap utilization periods coincide. If a currency is about to be devalued within a short time, swap possibilities decrease. Thus, e.g., in periods directly preceding the dollar devaluation, the Federal Reserve swap network temporarily ceased to function as nobody wanted to get dollars in exchange for his own currency.

Also due to their recompensating character, the so-called covered sale and purchase currency operations affect neither the central bank reserves nor the external monetary position, in which case a currency is bought for cash and the same currency is sold forward or the other way round. It is to be emphasized that these covered currency sale and purchase transactions, in contrast with swaps as mutual credit operations—which, as we have experienced do have an influence on the reserves, and moreover, their aim is precisely to increase them—affect neither the balance of payments nor the reserves. This is understandable as a cash currency purchase could have decreased central bank reserves but covered currency sales compensate such a decrease. As far as the balance of payments is concerned, covered currency sales are also indifferent, since a currency purchase increases external sight claims, while a currency sale against it, however, equally decreases them and vice versa.

The question arises as to why and for what purpose such covered currency operations come about, all the more as they represent a considerable share in the total currency transactions of the international banks. No doubt, they occur most frequently on account of their interest arbitration possibility. If the short-term interest rates are different in respect of the different currencies and if in respect of the premium or discount relating to the respective currencies do not reflect sufficiently this difference then, in order to make use of it, a currency purchase will take place. I would like to present an example to illustrate this point. Interest rate on the pound sterling is, say, 8 percent, and 5 percent on the dollar, then the sterling discount is 3.5 percent per annum. The bank with pound sterling stocks, which will be needed in the future, is interested in selling its sterling against the dollar and to repurchase it on forward base as the operation brings a profit, instead of the pound sterling with an 8 percent interest it will have the dollar bringing interest at 5 percent, which together with the premium (3.5 percent) interest earnings will increase to 8.5 percent.

Another factor giving rise to such covering operations is connected with banking activity itself or with the limitation of parallel risk. If a bank is instructed by one of its clients to buy on forward base foreign currency in larger amounts, then it buys it for itself as spot money. Banks generally follow this practice. There are countries like France where banks have to proceed this way by law. This is, however, changing the composition of their cash stocks in different currencies and for reestablishing it, banks generally have recourse to swap operations, which again involve compensated money movements. Finally, banks may wish to temporarily change the structure of their currency stocks with a view to their foreseeable needs and this is generally done through covering forward operations.

All these enumerated cases—in which a certain monetary transaction has no effect on the reserves, or on the real state of the balance of payments, i.e., on the external monetary position, and eventually on neither of them—are virtually exceptional and as we have seen they may be attributed either to time deferment, or to the compensating character of the operations. Nevertheless, the bulk of the currency operations are not liable to time deferment and are not of a compensating character. Thus, it has to be examined what influence uncovered currency operations have on reserves and on external monetary position. In such cases there is an obvious effect on reserves if sale and purchase take place in the domestic market. Influence on external finances is not so simple and is subject to various factors.

Within the circumstances of free foreign exchange management, those purchasing foreign currency either keep it, i.e., place it in their foreign exchange account with a domestic bank or give instruction to credit it in their favour with an external bank.

In the first case, in accordance with the above definition, a currency-purchase operation is indifferent from the point of view of external finances, since what happened is only that the purchased currency amount—finally decreasing central bank reserves—entered the banking system, or perhaps the safe of the buyer, but the total of the external public or private assets of the respective country did not undergo any change as long as the bought currency is used for external payments or lending.

The situation is different in the second case, when the buyer places the purchased foreign currency with an external bank. In that case central bank reserves decrease while the external currency stock of domestic banks does not increase. In accordance with the above definition of the external monetary position of a country—due to the decrease of the public and private foreign exchange total assets caused by the aforementioned foreign currency stock decrease—both the balance of payments and the external finances deteriorated, as the transaction in question was not covered, i.e., there was nothing on the other side of the balance sheet to offset the decrease.

In the case when there is foreign exchange control in the buyer country, which permits within certain limits foreign currency purchases but prohibits placing the purchased currency with an external bank, there is again no change in respect of the external finances. This case is, in fact, the same as the first alternative, although the purchased foreign currency remains within the country but not due to an autonomous decision of the buyer but in compliance with legal stipulations.

As far as lending operations are concerned, they are mostly uncovered or compensated. This is natural in respect of long-term currency loans as there is no market where their covering with forward operations could be possible. Uncovered currency loan operations equally affect central bank reserves of the respective countries, as—finally—such loans are granted to their debit while raising them increases the reserves, and also improve or damage their external monetary position, as at the time of either granting or taking the loans, as well as at their maturities they change the net balance of their obligations and claims.

We have to revert, however, to the uncovered currency sales and purchases, since sooner or later the aim of these operations is the utilization of the currency purchased, and due to their volume and frequency they have an influence on the whole functioning of the monetary system and thus affect all the elements intended to be regulated by the monetary system including the balance of payments, too, which is now our main topic. The major point of the market currency conversion, i.e., of the uncovered currency sale or purchase, is the price of the currency—the exchange rate. This develops primarily as a result of the combined effect of supply and demand, especially in the case of spot transactions. (Forward rates are also influenced by the future exchange rate orientation of the market.) This is why the net balance of payments and the external finances also influence the exchange rate as the negative balance reflects an excessive offer of the respective currency, while a surplus shows an excessive demand for it and, simultaneously, triggers off such a demand or supply, too. Therefore, the exchange rate of a certain country's currency and its balance of payments are in an interactive causal relationship, i.e., both affect the other.

Uncovered sale and purchase transactions have their impact on the balance of payments also through the domestic interest rate level. Namely, when the central bank buys foreign currency this involves the issuing of domestic currency and the consequent increase of the money supply has a lowering affect on domestic interest rate level. However, should the central bank sell the foreign currency, it will result, in turn, domestic currency inflows to the bank, lowering the volume of money supply and thus raising the domestic interest rate level. Buying a currency involves money issue, selling it means money withdrawal and both are followed by changes in interest rates. The attaining of higher interest yields being the major incentive for uncovered money movements—conversions—, interest rate level differentials orient demand, and, consequently, currency transactions, thereby influencing the direction of money flows, and hence they have an impact on the country's balance of payments.

To avoid any misunderstandings, it is to be emphasized that the pursuit of higher interest yields is only one of the motives for currency conversions. The other one is the market assessment of the cross exchange rate development of the different currencies. These two factors have opposite effect, as interest on weak currencies—precisely due to the fact explained above—is high, while that on strong ones is relatively low. It goes without saying that participants in the international short term money market transactions will prefer a definite currency because of its more advantageous interest yield inasmuch as the respective currency is not endangered by devaluation or by a considerable exchange rate decline in the near future. If, nevertheless, this is to be feared, then profitability considerations emanating from interest differences lose significance.

The following shall demonstrate this: If a 10 percent devaluation of a currency may be expected, then the interest yields of this currency should surpass by 120 percent for 1 month, by 40 percent for 3 months, and by 20 percent for 6 months that of the currency against which the devaluation-threatened ones would be purchased by someone, so that this purchase would be worthwhile from the aspect of profitability.

The balance of payments is compiled in the national currency of the individual countries and thus external currency obligations and claims expressed in domestic currency are influenced in their value by the exchange rate development of that currency in which claims and obligations prevail. From the point of view of the debtor's balance of payments it is advantageous, while from that of the creditor's it is unfavourable if the exchange rate of the respective currency declined since the drawing of the loan. Therefore, it is not indifferent in respect of the balance of payments position in which currency a certain country raises or grants a loan. For the sake of smoother international monetary relations this all would require more stable exchange rates which is, however, partly conditional on the equilibrium of the balances of payments.

As mentioned before, floating seemed applicable in principle to promote the automatic equilibrium of the balance of payments of at least the advanced industrial countries. This supposition was not unfounded, since if the currency of a certain country is floating, there is no intervention obligation and thus there are no consequences thereof, money flows calm down, because the exchange rate is determined by market demand and supply; the balance of payments equilibrium is established through the trade balance as depreciation automatically improves the latter, making imports more expensive.

These suppositions were not born out by experience. This is due not only to the fact that the possibility of floating did not exclude massive intervention at all, primarily precisely in favour of the dollar,* but is also due to many other factors. Besides the exchange rate, the balance-of-payments position is influenced also by other internal factors. Floating, if there really is no interven-

* From the beginning of February up to late April in 1980, i.e., during 3 months, central banks used $37 billion for intervention purposes first to prevent too high an upswing, and later the decline of the dollar (*Le Monde*, June 10, 1980.)

tion, does not affect those internal factors, only the exchange rate fluctuations and reserves. It is not our task here to monitor in detail the internal factors,* referred to above, which are in fact utilized by the states for influencing their balance of payments in the required way, as we shall see later, but nevertheless, in connection with the supposition of the automatic reestablishment of the balance of payments equilibrium through the trade balance, some of their aspects are worthy of attention.

It is also a matter of experience that between exchange rate modifications and trade balance positions there is less co-relation than previously supposed.† Factors of a non-price character have a large influence, and this was well shown by the fact that in the second half of the 70s the appreciation of the Deutsche Mark hardly influenced the German export volume. The time factor also has an impact: the effect of exchange-rate changes is delayed. This is interesting also for the reason as in case of really clean floating when exchange-rate fluctuations are presumably relatively smaller but frequent in volume, by the time the decrease or increase of the exchange rate could be felt in foreign trade, the exchange rate might have changed already reversely. Otherwise, the time factor does not always exert the same effect partly in the case of appreciation or depreciation, partly in the case of imports and exports: import prices immediately fall as a result of appreciation, thus appreciation instantly stimulates imports but its export-price-increasing influence could become effective only through hard price formation efforts.

Depreciation, on the other hand, has a faster effect both in respect of import price increasing, i.e., curtailing imports, as well as of stimulating exports. All this, however, is connected with the domestic price level, with the flexibility of supply and demand,

---

* See article by L. Gubcsi, "Fizetési mérleg elméletek" (Balance-of-payments theories), *Pénzügyi Szemle*, Nos 7-8, 1979.

† I. Szalkai: "Gondolatok a külső és belső egyensúly konfliktusairól" (Some reflections on external and internal equilibrium conflicts) (Internal study, Financial Research Institute, Budapest, 2/1980).

with the proportion of commodities participating in foreign trade turnover and of those belonging to the domestic non-competitive sector, but also with the domestic money supply and with the country's monetary and ecomonic policy—not to mention the eventual direct or indirect restrictions on international trade.

Those who expected from floating and from the automatic exchange rate changes exempted from the boundaries of fix parities the gradual equilibration of trade balances assumed that the opposite movements of cross rates would have an impact on prices and consequently on export–import volumes. The absence of these effects is attributed by the supporters of the so-called "asymmetry hypothesis"*—besides the above outlined factors—to the fact that price rises in countries with a depreciating currency are not counterbalanced by adequate price decreases in countries with an appreciating currency because wages and prices are not flexible downward. This conception is supplemented by the vicious circle theory according to which the devaluation of currencies is followed not only by the price rise of goods in foreign trade turnover, but also of all the totality of commodities, resulting in a general price level increase with the price–wage spiral starting to function.

It is not our task here to criticize hypotheses, even in respect of deciding whether the phenomena referred to in these theories—the downward inflexibility, the automatic functioning of the price–wage spiral which may be, no doubt, proved by examples of recent years' economic history—are normal and regular or only occasional. Still less is it our intention to examine what internal monetary and economic policy measures may be taken to avoid or moderate these phenomena. From our point of view, it is enough to repeat that exchange rate changes and floating designed to secure free exchange rate development did not prove suitable instruments for achieving the gradual equilibration of the payment balances. It is true, the real processes did not prompt in this direction, neither in respect of the actual trade balances, nor in respect of monetary aspects.

---

* Cf. Szalkai's previously quoted work.

Chapter III

Eurocurrency Markets

The problem of Eurocurrencies has been mentioned in the previous chapter in connection with the fact that the external monetary position of a country is seriously influenced by the quantities of foreign exchange originating from and going to the Euromarkets. The flow and accumulation of Eurocurrencies has become a significant factor in the international monetary system since it has an effect on the balance of payments—and thus on the external monetary position—of both the issuer and the user as well as the intermediary states. The existence of Eurocurrencies has a great influence on the reserves of the issuing central bank, too, because they come into being through the amounts of national currency which went abroad and were not exchanged, thus not reducing the reserves of the issuing central bank. There need not necessarily be any interconnection between the reserves of the central banks of the user and the intermediary countries, since the flows of Eurocurrencies do not automatically affect them. They do so only in the case when a Eurocurrency is converted into a national currency or vice versa. Therefore, one of our main preliminary lessons drawn from the examination of Eurocurrencies and Euromarkets is that in evaluating a country's external monetary position it is far from being enough to take into account only the trends of its monetary reserves. The importance of the flow of Eurocurrencies lies in the very fact that this flow is realized on special markets, essentially independent of the control of central banks. Therefore, we can speak in their case about an international monetary and financial market.

The aim of this chapter is to examine the laws of motion and the motives and circumstances of the emergence and development of these international money markets. Even if we wish to approach the question from the aspect of the market, we have also to make clear the concept and nature of the Eurocurrencies. The problems of the effects of the Euromarkets on the countries' external monetary position and those of its connections with the national money markets, as well as the examination of the channels through which they are realized, constitute the subject of further chapters.

It was mentioned already that if national currency outflows are not converted into another currency then a certain stock of them is piling up abroad. These currencies abroad are called Eurocurrencies, Euro-foreign exchanges. The latter indication is more accurate as these moneys represent claims against the central bank issuing the currency. The holders of Euro-foreign exchange amounts use them in short-, medium- or long-term lending. Thereby the credit market of the different Eurocurrencies is being created where credit transactions—and not just sales and purchases—take place. The Eurocurrency market is a credit market where the dominating factor is the interest rate evolution, not the exchange-rates. The exchange rates of a currency and its Euromarket interest level are, however, not independent of each other. Unless other factors influence them in the opposite direction, the interest levels of strong currencies are generally relatively low and those of weak ones are high. This is understandable, since in the case of weak currencies the exchange rate risk of the lender is higher, as he runs a higher risk of receiving a lower value at maturity than was lent. Higher interest is intended to compensate this larger exchange rate risk. This rule increasingly prevails in the Euromarket, where, as we shall see, interest level developments are not directly influenced by official measures. Notwithstanding, the Euromarket interest level is largely affected indirectly by the interest policy of the country issuing the respective currency, since placing the money in the domestic or in the Euromarket means alternative opportunities, and deciding upon one or the other depends not least on profitability.

Considering that the "Eurostock" in certain currencies unconverted into other ones is large enough, we have to deal thoroughly with the credit market of these Euromoneys, with the so-called Euromarket, the evolution, events and trends of which—due to the market volume and its rapid growth—influence the international money movements fundamentally and in various aspects. For the sake of completeness, before starting this detailed examination, the co-relation between the Euromarket and reserves is also to be examined. The relationship between them is inverse. Namely, the more domestic currency funds abroad are converted into other currencies, the less they remain in the Euromarket and reversely, the larger the extent to which a national currency outside the country is placed in the Euromarket, the less of it will be converted. This is why in a period when exchange rate speculation is keen, i.e., sales and purchases transactions are multiplied in the market, the reserves of the central bank, which is finally carrying out the conversions, will grow, and the Euromarket volume will decrease causing an upward interest level in the Euromarket. If, on the other hand, foreign exchange markets calm down with less conversions, the Euromarket volume will grow, exerting a reducing effect on interests.

We may also add that the impact on interests exerted by the supply side coincides with the direction exerted by the demand side. Currency speculation, in fact, generally feeds on borrowed money. Thus, in hectic monetary periods credit demand increases in the Euromarket, raising the interest level, while in calm periods demand declines, simultaneously lowering the interest level, too.

Returning to our actual topic, the Euromarkets, it is to be underlined above all that the use of the plural is not incidental but well justified. Firstly, because all domestic currencies outflowing in larger amounts and creating certain stocks abroad (US dollar, Deutsche Mark, etc.) have, in a sense, their separate credit markets. These markets influence each other; yet market conditions (primarily the interest) are different in respect of the individual currencies. These markets are the external parallel markets of the internal national money and capital credit markets and the parallel credit markets of the individual currencies taken as a whole are defined in the singular as Euromarket, which is in fact a collective noun.

Obviously, external stocks are not generated in all national currencies and consequently not each currency is in the Euromarket. The questions as to how and for what reasons the Euromarkets of the individual currencies are formed are ones which will be dealt with later more thoroughly. Let it suffice here to point out that only a convertible currency may have a parallel market of an important size. Contrary to other views, in my opinion the emergence of such a market is not conditional upon the full convertibility of the respective currency (this being anyway rather rare nowadays), but it is indispensable that the currency in question be regularly sold and purchased in bigger markets and that the issuer country ensure, at least for non-residents, the possibility of obtaining assets denominated in domestic currency and converting them into other national currencies, and, even if within certain boundaries for residents, to make transactions in external currencies. These conditions relate primarily to the formation of the market. Once a currency is in the Euromarket, any subsequent restrictions on these conditions cannot stop it but may only retard its development. (The French franc Euromarket, though smaller in volume, existed and functioned even in the early seventies when foreign exchange restrictions in France were the most severe.) The rule may be set so: the less restrictive the foreign exchange policy of a country is, the more possible it is for the external parallel credit market of its domestic currency to be formed.

The Euromarket, as a collective term, differs not only according to the various currencies but also in respect of maturities. Even one currency has two Euromarkets: the monetary and the financial, the short-term, as well as the medium-, and long-term credit market. The former, including all Eurocurrencies, is simply defined as Euro-foreign-exchange market, the latter often also Euro-issuing market as transactions in these markets are generally realized in the form of bond issues. These two markets are naturally not isolated from each other, but to the contrary, the relationship between them is strong and they differ rather in their technical aspects than in principles. Nevertheless, as they represent in fact two separate market-networks, it is justified to speak of them separately, although both are credit markets where the respective claims are not denominated in the lender's domestic currency. We are now mainly interested in the Euro-foreign-exchange markets, partly because speculation feeds on these markets and they are largely and dangerously influencing the functions and the security of the international monetary system.

It is not at all simple to assess the global volume of the Euromarkets as the relevant statistics contain estimates only. The survey is especially difficult as calculating net data, i.e., eliminating the repeated consideration of deposits may, as a matter of course, hardly be exact. In the aforequoted study, Szalkai takes as his base the data published in the *International Currency Review* (3/1979) where it is stated that the gross volume of Euromarkets at the end of 1978 was $860 billion, while the net volume was $480 billion. In an article by Paul Fabra published in *Le Monde* (September 29, 1979), also $860 billion is mentioned, based on March 1979 positions without defining whether it is a net or a gross volume.

In any case, and however reliable the "net" approach may be, it is certain that the Euromarket encompasses several hundred billion dollars. What this volume really represents may be assessed only if compared to the central bank reserves of the major Western industrial countries, or to the volume of money in circulation in the country. Comparison with reserves is interesting from the point of view of the above outlined relationship between Euromarket volume and currency amounts converted, but also for the reason that reserves represent means which are the best applicable by countries to safeguard against speculation on the depreciation of their currencies.

It is especially to be emphasized in this context that 70–80 percent of the global volume of the Euromarket supply consists of dollars. When comparing the volume of money already in the Eurodollar market with the one in circulation in the USA (based upon the data published by Szalkai and Fabra) we come to the result that in 1979 both the net and the gross Eurodollar amounts were already nearly the same or exceeded the internal money stock of the USA in the narrower and broader sense as well. The net Eurodollar volume was over the M_1—\$380 billion, the gross over the M_2—\$935 billion (*Time*, October 22, 1979). This alone proves that this Eurodollar volume, exactly because of the simultaneous key- and world-currency role of the dollar, has a decisive impact on the monetary system and on its concrete functioning.

It is worthwhile taking a look at the global growth rate of the Euromarkets. According to the above-mentioned data in 1970, the gross volume was \$110 billion, the net \$65 billion, which means that during eight years the volume grew eightfold. The annual average growth rate in this period was 28 percent, which itself is remarkable, the more because in 1977–1978 at the time of the repeated weakening of the dollar, this rate substantially accelerated. (In 1977, the gross volume was \$695 million, the net \$380 million as against \$860 and \$480 million in 1978 which has meant the highest ever growth rate both in volume and in percentage.)

For simplicity's sake, in the following we are going to deal mainly with the Eurodollar credit market, owing not only to the dominant share of the mentioned market, but also because this market was created first. National currency stock outflow to external countries did exist also prior to World War II and big banks concluded money transactions with each other in currencies other than either's domestic currency. The term "Eurocurrency", however, became generally accepted only at the beginning of the fifties and transactions in Eurocurrencies—at first almost exclusively in Eurodollars—started to grow in number only since those years. The effective Eurodollar credit market was getting established only in the second half of the fifties.

It seems likely that tensions caused by the Korean war led to certain dollar outflows towards Europe. Not wanting to have dollar funds deposited in Europe unused, European banks operated with them in the short-term money market. It was already frequently stated, though without proof, that "Korean" dollar outflows were primarily dollar amounts due to socialist countries and their enterprises since in that political atmosphere it was justly feared that they would be blocked. These dollars would have been deposited with one of the Paris banks (being in socialist ownership), the Banque Commerciale pour l'Europe du Nord, and this bank was the first initiator of large scale dollar transactions outside the territory of the USA. The telegraphic address of the bank "Eurobank", may have led to the term "Eurodollar". I tend to believe that dollars participating in European transactions were the first called Eurodollar, although this covers all dollars which are involved in transactions outside the territory of the USA. Later—*per analogiam*—also the terms Eurofranc, Euromark, etc. became widespread; in each case "Euro-" was prefixed to the currency which participated in the respective transaction.

From the above it is possible to see the major characteristics of the Eurodollar, and generally those of the Eurocurrencies, as well as of their markets. Speaking, for simplicity's sake, in dollar terms, they may be summarized in the following way:

1. The Eurodollar market is the market of claims denominated in dollars. Whenever such a claim is converted into another currency, we are no longer in the Eurodollar market. This does not mean that Eurodollars converted into other currencies could not return within a short time to the Eurodollar market, but only through a new conversion. These Eurodollars generally manifest themselves in the form of short-term deposits and sometimes in the form of sight deposits. Banks outside the USA grant dollar loans based on these deposits.

2. Eurodollar holders are not Americans, or rather, from the US viewpoint, they are non-residents. Most frequently, Eurodollars emerge in a way whereby US non-residents obtain foreign exchange claims vis-à-vis the USA either by purchasing dollars in the

market, or by not converting or not repatriating (i.e., not transferring to the USA) the countervalue of their sales against dollars (US sales are transacted almost exclusively against dollars), or in a way whereby US residents lend, generally out of their interest earnings, domestic dollars to non-residents. Irrespectively of how the Eurodollar emerged, its holder is always a non-resident.

3. The dollar funds in question are always deposited outside US territory. This exterritorial position (outside the dollar issuing country's territory) is the most important feature of the Eurodollar's role. Therefore, it mihgt be better to speak not of the Eurodollar market but of the dollar market outside US territory, since the delimiting factor against the "domestic" dollar is just the market where dollar transactions take place, and not the fact that these transactions are effected in dollars.

4. Eurodollars are always utilized outside the US territory. They immediately loose, however, their "Euro" character as soon as they are utilized in the USA or are repatriated thereto on account of settling some other obligation or lending to residents.

Finally, if the definitions of the Eurodollar are generalized, the meaning of "Euro" may be interpreted simply but rightly in such a way that it involves all bank deposits which are not denominated in the domestic currency of the bank where they were deposited.

It may be useful to present a hypothetical example to illustrate the actual functioning of the Eurocurrency markets. Let us suppose—and this assumption is more typical than it seems at first sight—that a British bank where a French bank has deposited dollars makes a loan to a German bank, which then lends them to a Japanese importer intending to buy from Germany. Should all this happen for a short term, these (monetary) actions are effected in the Euromarket, but if the depositor (the French bank in this case) had intended to use the deposit for medium- or long-term financing, and the final user, in this case the Japanese enterprise, borrowed the money also with the same intention, then the above described range of operations is to be considered as an activity affecting the international financial money market—where usance conditions are different. The delimiting factor, consequently, is the intention of the lender and of the beneficiary in respect of the credit maturity mostly stipulated in their respective agreements.

After the broad outlines of the Euromarket operations, we have to deal more thoroughly with the basic reasons behind the creation of the Euromarket, and primarily of the Eurodollar market. The adjective "basic" is to be emphasized as it is obvious and natural that not only one reason but also other ancillary reasons and circumstances—on both the demand and the supply side—as well as quite a range of the market; some of them in respect of the long-term Eurodollar market, and further ones regarding the other currencies' markets.

No one disputes that Eurodollars stemmed from the US's balance of payments deficit. Had this balance been in equilibrium, payment obligations to be met by non-residents vis-à-vis the USA would have absorbed the entire dollar amount deposited abroad. Eurodollars were emerging precisely due to the reason that more dollars left the USA than returned to it. The lasting US balance-of-payments deficit could not be feasible but in the context of such an international monetary approach which made the dollar the basis of the monetary system—the dollar which is virtually the unique key currency, which the USA was practically unwilling to convert either into gold, or into other currencies, though legally this had been possible until August 15, 1971. Thus, the emergence of Eurodollars was strongly related to the Bretton Woods international monetary system which made possible the steady and increasing deficit of the US balance of payments. However, the fact that dollar funds that had left the US in the mentioned way formed an effective market and that this market gained such an important role is connected only indirectly with the lasting US balance-of-payments deficit. In this context, besides the advantages of flexibility offered by the Eurodollar market (to be dealt with later), it is to be emphasized as a basic reason that the dollar continues to play a decisive role in the international trade and financial transactions, not only as a key currency but also as a transaction tender in which the major part of the trade and financial transactions of the Western world is carried out, but with the significant contribution of the Eurodollar market.

The existence of the Eurodollar market absorbing the dollars stemming from the US's balance-of-payments deficit facilitated for the USA as debtor to continuously maintain its deficit position. Without the Eurodollar market—meaning that external dollars would be less available—there would have been much greater pressure on the US to reestablish its balance-of-payments equilibrium and it would have had to reckon already in the mid-sixties with the consequences of the dangerous depletion of its reserves. Thus the existence of the Eurodollar market and the outstandingly rapid growth of its volume delayed and continues to delay the necessary reform of the monetary system which makes the *status quo* bearable for the USA.

The rapid development of the short-term Eurodollar market was also furthered by the temporarily applied US monetary regulations of a restrictive character which oriented short-term funds from the domestic credit market, which promised less profits, to the Euromarket. Such was the so-called "Q regulation" which, based upon the cheap money theory and for the sake of the reactivation of economic life and also in favour of medium banks with difficulties in the interest competition, restricted interests to be paid on deposits. (It is possible that taking these restrictive measures was also induced by the intention to develop the Euromarkets as this was in compliance with US interests at that point. What is certain is that in the summer of 1970, when they wanted the dollar outflow curtailed, this regulation was withdrawn.)

Other internal US credit restrictions also promoted the Eurodollar market. While the Q regulation increased Euromarket offer, these credit restrictions curtailing external and later internal lending, also stimulated an upward trend in the Euromarket demand, since external borrowers were compelled to face the Euromarket, instead of the US domestic market and US banks acted accordingly too, raising sizable dollar loans in the Euromarket.

Finally, some circumstances of a technical nature on the demand side contributed as well to advance the market, such as the difference between the crediting and debiting practice of the bank accounts in the USA and the so-called Federal Funds. If a US bank raised a certain dollar amount in the Euromarket on, let us say, a Thursday morning, this was credited in its favour through the clearing house that same evening. It was possible already on Friday to repay the amount to the debit of its account kept with the Federal Reserve Bank, but the respective debit entry on the account was effected only with Monday's value. The bank in question could thus equilibrate its balance position as stipulated by the authorities for three days at the cost of one day's Eurodollar market rate. Another technicality, on account of which the large volume of the Eurodollar market was advantageous, was that the structure of their passives was certainly not indifferent for the US banks because they were compelled to create non-interest earning reserves with the central bank in proportion with their deposits. Such an obligation was not involved in respect of loans raised on the Euromarket. From the technical points of view, the Euromarket also has the advantage of stabilizing deposits. If a bank has a sight foreign exchange deposit—and this is the most frequent form—it is not known for how long the volume of money represented by the deposit would be at disposal, while raising a loan in the Euromarket means a maturity known well in advance.

As far as medium- and long-term Eurodollar capital markets are concerned, their emergence was largely promoted by the "equalization tax" introduced in the USA in 1964, and designed to cut back capital flow and thus to increase demand on the Euro-capital-market. This tax (cancelled in 1974) raised the interest burden on medium- and long-term loans granted abroad by 1 percent, the buying of foreign shares became 15 percent more expensive, and that of bonds (depending on their lifetimes) went up by 2.75–15 percent. (The longer maturity a bond had, the higher was the taxation.) As a result of the "equalization tax", demand for medium- and long-term credits, which up to that time could be primarily met in the USA, had to leave the American capital market, more or less at the same time when Great Britain was also compelled to restrict its external lendings from her reserves.

This is already past history. What is more recent is the flow of unused dollar surplusses of the petroleum producing countries to the Euromarkets, especially to the short-term Euromarket, which is, for the time being, the main characteristic of the growing volume, considering that in the second half of the seventies the majority of the dollar outflows from the USA augmented not so much the Euromarkets, but—being converted—rather the central bank holdings.

The increase in Euromarkets volume caused by petro-dollars, contrary to the dollar outflows from the USA, stems not from the balance-of-payments deficit, but precisely from balance surplusses. The same was the situation with the other Eurocurrency markets (Euromark, Eurofranc, etc.) as well when the capital export of countries with active balances of payments represented the basis of the external currency stocks and consequently of their market, too. Therefore, it is not essential from the point of view of the parallel market and its further development whether the balance of payment position of the issuing country shows a deficit or a surplus; what is important is that money outflows take place to some extent and more or less continuously and that the money involved not be converted. Non-conversion of the domestic currencies is possible only when they may be profitably used for the purpose of lending operations abroad. (The dollar's case is, in fact, special, and this may be attributed to its privileged position in the monetary system since this is why the dollar may be used abroad, despite the fact that the balance of payments of the issuing country shows a deficit and its outflow is not fed on surplusses, but just the contrary, on deficit.)

But what is that particular advantage of parallel credit markets which in fact made their formation possible? It is primarily the fact that they are free and unlimited, not restricted by government regulations. Euromarket interest rates fluctuate freely according to the rules of supply and demand. (The interest level of the country issuing the respective currency influences the development of supply and demand.) Failing such regulations, the obligatory reserve formation does not increase the costs of the banks. Euromarkets generally enjoy a favourable position from the points of view of taxes as well, partly because those countries which intend to promote the existence of Euromarkets in their territory grant certain tax preferences, but also—as these markets are, as a matter of course, much more adequate than the domestic ones—in order to ensure the anonymity of currencies participating in the credit turnover. These circumstances also led the big multinational enterprises to increasingly enter these markets. Their steadily growing significance enhanced the Euromarket demand which, as well known, always generates supply. This is also an essential reason for the increase of the Euromarket volumes.

Thus, it may be said that Euromarket centres developed in those countries where use of the above-mentioned advantages is allowed to be made more freely or indulgently and to the maximum extent. The individual countries are making endeavours in this direction as Euromarket transactions yield considerable receipts of commissions for the participating banks of the country where the transactions are effected without the curtailment of the domestic money market and the decrease of central bank holdings.

London is the most important Euromarket center since the sixties. Wishing to maintain the leading role of the London Euromarket with all the advantages involved, Great Britain definitely opposes the introduction of rules in respect of the Euromarket control. Zürich ranks second in Europe, but Frankfurt and Paris are also seeking to carve out their share in the Euromarket operations. Luxembourg and also Liechtensein have a certain role in respect of issues as they provide very favourable tax conditions. In recent times, Euromarket centres have developed in other parts of the world as well, like Hong-Kong, Singapore, the Bahamas, etc.

Otherwise, it may be seen virtually as a rule that the less the domestic currency of a country participates in external credit operations, the more the respective country is fit to become a market of Euro-transactions.

The advantages stemming from the freedom and lack of restrictions entail, however, certain drawbacks, too, like, for example, the higher lending risks since Euroloans may not be mobilized at any of the central banks. Furthermore, due to the mobile and varied Euromarkets it is often difficult to assess the goodwill of the final debtor. It is for this reason that the idea emerged in West-European countries interested in the market to establish a mutual credit insurance company, but this is yet to be realized.

To a certain extent the US banking system as such plays, however, the same role in the Eurodollar market as the central bank in the domestic credit markets. Namely, if there are difficulties in the market, US banks are approached since by means of the "domestic" dollar such difficulties may be overcome. Mention should also be made of the regulating role played by the BIS in the Eurodollar market, which—with a view to keeping interests at a normal level—intervenes from time to time, but regularly in this market. It is a year-end and mid-year practice of certain European banks—mainly German and Swiss—to achieve a "window-dressing" effect, wishing to show a considerable liquidity position in domestic currencies, to withdraw their money deposited in the Eurodollar market and to convert it into their domestic currency so that supply strongly declines in the market and the interest rate increases accordingly. In such cases the BIS intervenes, not in order to change the market trend, but to reduce the temporary fluctuation, endeavouring partly to induce its shareholders to market-alimentation, partly to increase supply in the Eurodollar market by way of "domestic" dollars put up by the Federal Reserve System. In this case, too, domestic dollar is transformed into Eurodollar and this is the exceptional case when Euromarket requirements lead to the creation of money within the territory of the USA.

The Euromarket lender naturally also runs the risk, at least in theory, that in the period between the granting and the maturity of the credit the debtor's country might prohibit its repayment in the respective currency, or does not transfer it. According to experience, however, this danger exists more in theory than in practice; in any case, aside from the hardly likely overall monetary collapse, it is of an individual character.

The ever increasing role of the Eurocurrency market involves certain risks not only from the point of view of the lenders, but also mainly and to a much greater degree, from the point of view of the independence and sovereignty of the economc policy of the respective countries. One of the most effective economic policy means is credit policy, but the possibilities of the individual countries in the field of credit policy are, however, strongly influenced by the existence of the Eurocurrency market and its considerable volume. This is effected already through the extension of the borrowing possibilities—the so-called credit basis—considering that the Euromarket offers by all means an alternative against domestic credit possibilities. Apart from this, the Euromarket and the domestic interest rate levels of a certain currency, due to the above mentioned reasons inevitably interfere with each other in both directions, that is, not only the domestic interest rate level affects the Euromarket one, but also vice-versa. If the Euromarket interest rate level is high, it is rather difficult to keep it relatively low in a country participating in the Euromarket and vice versa. The only protection against it may be the introduction of foreign exchange restrictions, or at least government control of money movements. However, experience indicates that this otherwise preferred remedy does not prove efficient either.

The central banks of the various countries try to influence the Euromarket. They generally do not intervene themselves, but through those commercial banks of their country which are active in the Euromarket. When the Bundesbank—due not so much to interest yield considerations, but rather to having deemed its dollar holdings as sufficient and unwilling to buy US government securities to a larger extent, and also due to political reasons unable to convert its dollars into gold—put sizable dollar amounts at the disposal of the German banks, it was well aware of the fact that they would be placed in the Euromarket, and when the Banque de France borrowed dollars from the French banks, their Euromarket origin was also known to it. All these operations represent certain forms of intervention. The intervention character was more emphasized by the fact that the Bundesbank guaranteed for the German banks for a longer period (1968–1969) the parity of the dollars lent to them vis-à-vis the Deutsche Mark, thus undertaking the risk of the eventual revaluation of the DM. Central banks have recourse also to a certain pressure on their banks so that they behave at the Euromarket as expected. The most typical example in this respect is Italy. In 1964, the Banca d'Italia, seeking to maintain a certain liquidity in the country urged to the Italian banks to become debtors in the Euromarket. In spring 1969, also upon the advice of the central bank, Italian banks withdrew a considerable part of their Euromarket deposits. It is true anyway, that the relevant advice was duly supported by the interest rate policy of the central bank which made domestic money more expensive.

Reverting to the impact the Eurocurrency market has on domestic economies, it is to be emphasized that the existence of the Euromarket increases borrowing opportunities. As a result of the existence of the Euromarket, credit operations to some extent got beyond the control of the central banks, and the greater borrowing opportunities caused difficulties in the application of restrictive domestic credit policy which was to be continued eventually. It is obvious, too, that the internal monetary policy of the USA, the issuing country of the most important Eurocurrency, increasingly influences the internal finances and economies of the countries involved in the Eurodollar market. In fact, the steady increase of the Eurodollar volume stemmed partly precisely from the difference between the lending rate levels in the US domestic market and the Euromarket, the difference at that time being in favour of the Euromarket.

The employ of government measures to influence the internal interest level may also serve as a means of influence in respect of the interest rates of the parallel market, i.e., of the respective currency. This is a more direct means in contrast to the above-mentioned ones affecting the direction of the money flows, i.e., on the market volume. The utilization and the effects of this means will be dealt with later.

Although, considering its volume and growth rate, the short-term Euromarket is of much higher importance, some characteristics of the long-term Euromarket are also worthy of attention. There are no restrictions in these markets, which, besides its several advantages, has also some drawbacks from the lender's point of view. The disadvantages cannot be felt so much in the so-called primary market, i.e., in the long-term money market in the course of the issues, but rather in the secondary market, when the holder of a Eurobond intends to mobilize, to sell it. Although certain Eurobonds are quoted on several important stock exchanges, these quotations, due to the relatively small turnover, are less authentic and do not mean that the respective security could really be sold at the price quoted.

In the case of Eurocurrency issues, such operations being long-term ones, the choice of the currency of the issue, i.e., in which the loan is granted, is especially decisive, as, from the lender's security point of view (security holders), currency stability is of primary importance, which is just opposite the debtor's interests. Issues are, however, most frequently in dollars due to its leading role in international economic relations. Swiss authorities are not so much in favour of Swiss franc emissions, thus, besides the dollar Deutsche Mark issues are the most common, though the reinforcement of the dollar and the weakening of the DM decreased the number of DM issues. Alternative issues took place, too, with an option of two currencies, such as, e.g., sterling and Deutsche Mark. In such cases, the lender may, at maturity claim the due capital and interest amount in the currency of his choice. Finally, mention is to be made of issues in "units of account". These are based either on the currencies of the seventeen member countries of the past EPU, or recently, on the unit of account of the EMS (the ECU). No doubt, in principle, these issues seem to be the most perfect, nevertheless, the wider financial community, maybe on account of the complications involved, has yet to become thoroughly familiar with them. A deeper examination of their mechanism is beyond our subject, but it should be remarked that these alternative issues generally have valorization in mind.

The co-relation between short-term and long-term Euromarkets is of the same character as the normally developed relation between the domestic monetary and financial money markets. The higher the interest level is in the monetary market, the higher the proportionate volume of the short-term deposits grow—to the detriment of the capital market placements. Even disregarding this, the Eurocurrency market is strongly influenced by the bond market, as funds returning at maturity and prior to being utilized again are remporarily placed in the Eurocurrency markets, i.e., they increase the volume of the Eurocurrency market. Interest rates prevailing in the bond markets are also affecting the Eurocurrency market, since—especially at the time of monetary crises—when long-term placements are less preferable, the Eurocurrency market offers certain alternatives for capital tending otherwise toward the Eurobond market, because in such cases—since for short-term speculation on parity changes no interest rate is too high—short-term lending rates go higher than long-term ones, while in the logical way the interest level should be higher in respect of long-term credits. (This phenomenon is called "twist" after the once popular dance and is always considered the signal of crisis.) On the other side, interest rates in the Eurocurrency market have an influence on the Eurocapital market also because managers and intermediate banks in bond issues—as long as the bond amounts taken will have been placed—temporarily cover themselves in the Eurocurrency market.

At this stage a bit more ought to be said about the so-called maturity transformation in respect of the Euromarket. This means in fact the transformation of the maturities, more clearly, the damaging and dangerous case when a bank uses short-term money for medium- and long-term lending. Such a transaction, the temptation of which, due to lack of supervision, is rather high in the Euromarket, is dangerous enough, and in stricter banking terms, especially when it is not of an isolated nature, because naturally it considerably reduces the bank's liquidity and it is harmful since it endangers the money market stability. Banks are tempted to transform maturities just for interest rate considerations. The rate of interest on medium- and long-term loans is generally not determined in fix percentages but is adjusted by revision every half year to the London Interbank Offered Rate for 6-month Eurodollar deposits (roll over basis) in a way so that the interest will be higher by a certain margin. Banks are motivated to make such placements of their short-term assets by this interest margin and by the adjustment to the short-term interest rate of any time, although during the relatively long lifetime of the loan the financial standing of the debtor may weaken. Maturity transformation is especially risky, if, on the contrary, the bank lends at a fixed interest rate, and refinances the loan on a roll over basis. In such cases, in addition to the debtor's standing the interest level may also change intensively and, consequently, the risks may increase to an impermissible extent.

Dealing with the phenomenon of the maturity transformation, which frequently occurs in the Euromarket and thus endangers the security of the credit turnover, leads us almost involuntarily to the much disputed question of whether the existence of the Euromarket and its rapid growth rate entail money supply or only redistribute money. This is not only a question of principle, as it may be put in another way: do the Euromarkets have an inflationary impact? If the so-called Eurobanks operating in these markets do not respect the general rules of credit security this will result, as was pointed out before, in unhealthy and inflationary credit expansion. Thus, the question to be answered is whether, even in the case of compliance with wise bank stipulations, an additional money supply would emerge as a result of the functioning of the Euromarket.

Before examining this point, let's have a look at credit security. The most essential assurance in this respect is the creation of reserves, which is a natural prerequisite of banking activity designed for the bank to have the necessary liquid assets to meet its payment obligations at any time even if, due to some reason, the latter grow more than usual. (Depositors destabilize the bank.) Obviously, banks want to keep their holdings at a low level if possible, since they bring small profits (less than the credits granted), or nothing at all where the compulsory reserves to be placed with the central bank are concerned. The ratio between the global amount of deposits and that of the bank's liquid assets is generally called the "multiplier".

Euromarkets being free of and beyond central bank control have no compulsory stipulations concerning reserves, and the multiplier itself is not defined by anyone, being only dependent on the decision of the respective Eurobank. It may be assumed, though not proved, that banks are more liberal in this respect vis-à-vis the Euromarkets than the local markets which are compulsorily regulated. According to general practice, Eurobanks place their reserves in the form of sight deposits with one of the banks of the issuing country of the respective currency, and thus Eurodollar holdings, being the most significant due to the size of the Eurodollar market, are placed with a bank in the USA. This is an essential factor as we shall see later.

Even assuming that Eurobanks act with the necessary caution in respect of the reserves, Euromarkets, like any other money markets,* do have a certain—though more or less restricted—money making ability as a result of the well-known phenomenon of

---

* Article by Milton Friedman in *Morgan Guaranty Survey* October 1969.

"loans make deposits", thus duplication and its inflationary effect may not be considered insignificant.

It may be understood, consequently, that relatively early, at the very beginning of the sixties, there arose the issue of controlling and regulating the Euromarkets to a certain extent and the larger these markets grew in volume the more urgent the issue became. Of course, finding the right solution is not simple due to various reasons. First of all because the major advantage of the Euromarkets lies precisely in their being unrestricted, which is hard to reconcile with regulation and control. However, in the interest of world trade and financing balance-of-payment deficits, it is especially important that adequate liquid assets be available. Such liquid means are mainly produced by the Euromarkets and thus several countries, also including the socialist countries, are interested in leaving these markets unrestricted by regulating and supervising rules.

Nor are those countries interested in the strict regulation of the Euromarket, whose banks take an active part in these markets as intermediaries (like Britain), and besides, how could such regulation be effected: by the countries of the economic units participating on an international level, or in the market as creditor or debtor, or perhaps by the issuing country of the currency in the Euromarket of which credit operations are transacted? If it is decided that the "home countries" of the Eurobanks are to exercise control, then how would it be assured that the respective stipulations be equally observed by banks in the Bahamas and Singapore, for example, as by their London counterparts?

Chapter IV

Interconnections among the National Money Markets and their Relationship to the Euromarkets (International Money Flows)

Having defined some fundamental concepts and given a review of the Euromarkets, we shall now examine the interconnections among the national money markets and their relationship to the Euromarkets, which is the main focus of this study. Although some countries participating in the international monetary system maintain, in principle, the system of free movement of money and capital, in practice, certain restrictions and regulations exist in every country; it may be said that the examination of the phenomena indicated in the title of this chapter is nothing else but the examination of existing restrictions on the freedom of international money and capital flows.

Nevertheless, it seems necessary to deal first with the above interrelations from a certain theoretical approach, and to point out the practical restrictions only afterwards. These restrictions can take essentially two forms: those which mean a certain limitation on capital movements in a free foreign exchange system, and therefore do not affect the current (commercial, etc.) money flows and those which are a consequence of exchange control itself, since this covers by definition more or less strictly all international money and capital flows. We shall deal with these two categories separately, although in practice they may appear in various shades, and the dividing line between them can hardly be drawn.

*

The individual national—domestic—money markets are linked by the money and capital flows. In this respect, the Euromarkets—as international money markets—fall under the same category as any other foreign money market. The examination of the interrelations among the national money markets themselves consists, therefore, in the study of international money and capital movements. What do we call international money flow? All operations in consequence of which national or foreign currency possessed by an individual or a legal entity is being transformed into another currency. If someone, for example, possesses French francs and buys dollars or any other foreign currency with it for any reason or purpose, an international money movement takes place.

It should be noted in parentheses that, following from what was said in the previous paragraph, if someone simply borrows from the Euromarket, this, in itself, does not correspond to the definition given above, since in this case there is no money movement—at least for the time being—because there has been no currency exchange. Therefore, the expression, which we used previously in its generally adopted sense, namely, that the US companies "repatriate capital" when borrowing from the Euromarket, is in fact inaccurate, since in this case no conversion takes place, or at best only in the sense that by repatriation the Eurodollar loses its "Euro" character and turns temporarily into domestic dollar.

Money movements can be of two types: uncovered and covered with a forward operation. An uncovered money flow is unidirectional, i.e., it takes place when a currency is bought or sold, namely, one currency is being exchanged for another. If at the same time there is a defined term forward reciprocal deal, we may speak about covered money movement. Thus, we speak about a forward covered money movement if, taking our previous example, someone buying dollars for French francs, in order to cover himself against risk, makes the reciprocal transaction at the same time, namely, buys francs to be delivered later at a fixed date, as a counterpart for the previously bought dollars.

The difference between covered and uncovered money flows is of *decisive importance* from our point of view, since, we saw that only the uncovered money movements influence the balance of payments and the external monetary position, as well as the central bank reserves of a country, thereby affecting the spot exchange rate of the national currency and its interst rate, too. Covered money movements are neutral from these aspects.

As far as the interests are concerned, it has to be mentioned that in this chapter under the term "interest" we always mean short-term interests since the money flows affect these primarily and almost exclusively. Long-term interest rates are much more dependent on the general economic and investment climate, the volume of credit, etc. of the debtor's country. On the other hand, as far as long-term capital movements are concerned, they can be considered as uncovered money flows since there is no market where there would be a possibility to cover them on term, unless—exceptionally—they are covered on the short-term market with permanent renewals of the covering operations.

The fact that covered money movements have no effect on the external financial position and the reserves has already been thoroughly examined. Here only their impact on the exchange rates and interests—also of a neutral nature—has to be dealt with. As far as spot rates are concerned, they are not affected by the covered money movements, because a simultaneous and equal supply and demand situation occurs on the market. How does this occur? It is best illustrated by an example. A London company possessing pound sterling intends to buy Deutsche Mark covering itself forward. To get DMs it will first of all sell its pound sterling, thus creating an offer of pounds on the spot foreign exchange market. Then, as it wants to cover itself, it gives an order to its bank to buy (back) the same amount of pound sterling for a three-month period. The bank, acting on this order, buys immediately, i.e., against cash, the given amount and keeps it as long as it has to deliver it to the client. Thus, in the cash market there arises a demand for pound sterling as a consequence of the covering purchase. This means that, on the one side, pound sterling was sold, and, on the other, that pound sterling was purchased by the bank which carried out the covering purchase.

Finally, as far as the effect of the covered money movements on the interest level of the given currencies is concerned, one can say it is non-existent. These money flows—as we have seen—influence neither central bank reserves, nor the quantity of money in circulation in the countries concerned, on which the interest level finally depends. The issue of money withdrawal—thus the expansion of restriction of the quantity of money in circulation—occurs only if the central banks buy or sell foreign currency; as a matter of fact, owing to the compensating character of covered capital flows, this does not actually happen; respective purchases and sales counterbalance each other.

*

The case is quite different with uncovered international money flows. Before going into details concerning their manifold influence, we have to examine the reasons behind and the factors leading to the conversion of one currency into another. The first and most important reason lies obviously in international trade. Namely, if someone buys goods for foreign currency but has none in his possession, he has to buy it in order to meet his obligations towards the seller, that is, to be able to pay for the goods. If, on the contrary, he did not buy, but has sold goods for foreign currency, it depends on him barring rules to the contrary—whether he keeps the price received in the foreign exchange in question, or sells it for another, perhaps for his own national currency. In his decision, besides other business considerations, the expectation about the given currency's future parity, or if there is not any, then its exchange rate will also play an important role, as well as its yield (the interest it brings). Thus, such a decision contains speculative elements, too. But even purchase in a foreign currency is not exempt from such elements, since in the case of freely convertible currencies—and the lack of exchange control—the buyer often may choose the currency in which he buys, as it is also not by chance in which currency the seller stipulates the price. The more uncertain the international monetary situation is, the more strongly do these speculative elements assert themselves.

However, when looking at money movements that are independent of the flow of goods, I myself would unquestionably put purely speculative reasons in the first place. Events on the foreign exchange market in recent years, when we could experience the size and the frequency of uncovered speculative money movements, justifies this. Whenever the possibility of revaluation or devaluation—or when floating, a significant change in the exchange rate of currency—was likely in the near future, the volume of the sales of the currency arousing suspicions of devaluation or a sharp fall in its exchange rate, and the volume of buying of the currency to be supposedly revalued, or the exchange rate of which is supposed to rise, sharply increased. In such a situation, speculators buy "strong" currency with the "weak" currencies they either have or have borrowed and try to gamble on both possibilities of upward and downward changes in value.

Speculation arises from actual facts which have concrete economic foundations; these facts make speculation possible, and, if the speculator's judgement is sound, lucrative. The term "speculation" can be used not only in a pejorative, but also in another sense, meaning the estimation of probable future tendencies for the purpose of profit-making, and as such, it is the concomitant of all capitalist commercial activity. As money—and especially foreign exchange—is also a commodity, it is natural that those trading in it, primarily banks, want to gain a profit on it. The most significant gain can be reached through a change in parities, which is why such speculation shows the greatest volume. This speculation is provoked by those in the international foreign exchange market who believe that the parity of one or another currency is inappropriate. The most characteristic symptom of this is when the parity does not correspond to the real purchasing power of the currency in question, which may be a result of many causes, but its gauge is the balance-of-payments position of the issuing country. The speculative motive can, of course, assert itself in the case of floating currencies, too, but speculation in this case is not directed to changing the parity, but "only" the exchange rate which can easily and frequently be of the same size as the change of parity in the case of a currency with fixed rate.

The second reason is not purely speculative, but rather precautious in character, aiming to cover certain trade and financial risks that have existed previously. This operation, called hedging (restriction of risks), is especially frequent when the situation on the foreign exchange markets becomes uncertain. A very good example of this was when at the first news of a possible revaluation of the Deutsche Mark, a number of big foreign companies (from a German aspect) with DM obligations rushed to cover themselves and bought Marks, lest later they should have to meet their obligations at a higher cost. Such hedging is possible from the seller side, too. If someone has securities denominated in a foreign exchange liable to devaluation and cannot or does not want to sell them, he avoids the devaluation risk by borrowing in the same currency and the selling the amount that has come into his possession this way.

Undoubtedly, uncovered international money movements can be provoked not only by purely economic but also by psychological security considerations. International capital seeks security above of all and is obviously reluctant to make placement in countries where there is even just a hint of danger to security. A very characteristic example of the anxiety of mobile capital was when events in Czechoslovakia in August 1968 brought about a serious outflow of capital from Europe to the USA. Among other factors, this situation also played an important role in the fact that the US balance of payments showed a surplus the same year. When the shock psychosis was over, the flood back to Europe started—now for interest reasons—and this was one of the elements of the complex causes leading later to changes in parities. Similarly, the capital flows from Italy and France starting in recent years—as a consequence of a swing to the Left or only of the possibility of the same—mainly to Switzerland as an interim station, can be attributed also to the security-seeking tendency of mobile capital.

Under normal circumstances, the most frequent reason for uncovered money movements is the search for the most favourable interest conditions, which means speculation on the changes in the interest rate levels. It can be also mentioned that money flows started in order to gain higher interest returns may reach such an extent which already brings about changes in value, that is, it can turn into speculation on revaluation or devaluation, coming about either *de jure* or *de facto*. However, usually, if the banks do not consider a positive change in the value of a currency with a low interest return probable, they will exchange their stock of the given currency into another with higher interest, unless they fear the depreciation of the later currency. The West-German Bundesbank was led by the same consideration when it preferred to keep the bulk of its reserves in dollars rather than in gold, because by placing them the interest returns amply covered the then small risk of a possible dollar devaluation.

Uncovered money movements take place in practice either in the form of a spot exchange—namely, if the buyer has cash at his disposal—or as a forward deal. In the latter case, the purchase is financed not by the buyer himself but by the bank which has the buyer's order. Serious banks involved in international money flows usually conclude covered deals. They often play some role in carrying out uncovered deals, but generally not for their own account. If they do so nonetheless, it can have highly embarrassing consequences in case they misjudge the tendency of the currency constituting the subject of their deal. There were a number of examples in the mid-seventies when inappropriate forward currency speculation caused serious losses to significant, well-known banks.

Now let us examine the effects of uncovered money flows. The effect exerted on the spot exchange rates of the currencies and on the central bank reserves is obvious. As far as the exchange rates are concerned, they develop according to supply and demand. As in the case of the uncovered money flows, there is no covering offer against the demand and vice versa; the free movement of the exchange rate, at least within the intervention points (if there are any in case the given currency has fixed parities), is not obstructed. Concerning reserves, I would like to refer to a personal experience. During the second half of the sixties, at the time of the currency crisis preceding the revaluation of the DM and the devaluation of the French franc, I was living in France. Expecting the franc's devaluation, well-informed companies and individuals alike bought dollars and the exchange rate of the dollar reached the upper intervention limit. The Banque de France—owing to its intervention obligation—was compelled to supply the market with dollars against francs. As a consequence, its reserves dropped with alarming speed. Those, however, who deserted the franc, bought dollars in order to purchase DM and converted their dollars into DM at German banks. The banks, also expecting the revaluation of the DM, handed the dollars they obtained this way over to the Bundesbank, thereby increasing the latter's reserves.

We should note here that at the same time when the exchange rates of the French franc, the pound sterling, the Belgian franc, and the lire sank to their lower intervention point due to their ample supply and that of the Deutsche Mark ran high, the rate of exchange of the Swiss franc remained stable. The reason was that although people expected the revaluation of the Swiss currency and therefore a great amount of Swiss francs flowed into Swiss banks, these banks themselves expected the revaluation of the Mark and placed the incoming money in Deutsche Marks. The stability of the Swiss franc was due to this two-way money movement.

The effect of uncovered money flows on the balance of payments and the external monetary position of a country is more complicated and depends on several factors. If there is no exchange control, someone buying foreign currency either takes it in possession, i.e., places it in his foreign exchange account at his home bank, or gives an order to put the amount to his credit at a foreign bank. In the former case, according to the definition given above, the purchasing operation is irrelevant from the aspect of the external monetary position since only the obtained foreign exchange—which in the end decreased the central bank reserves—goes to the banking system or perhaps to the buyer's safe, but the total of the country's foreign public and private claims—and thus that of the balance of claims and obligations—does not change.

The situation is different in the second case, when the buyer places the foreign currency at a foreign bank. In that case the central bank reserves decrease but the foreign currency stock of home banks do not increase. By our definition of a country's external monetary position, as a consequence of the fall in the foreign exchange stock and given the country's decreasing total public and private foreign claims, the balance of payments and the external monetary position worsened since there was no counterpart compensating factor for the decrease because the deal was uncovered.

However, in the case when there is foreign exchange control in the buyer's country, which may permit the purchase of foreign currency within certain limits but bars the placement of foreign exchange at a foreign bank, again there is no change concerning the external monetary position. This case is, in fact, identical with the previous one, although the bought foreign currency remains within the country not because of the buyer's decision but because of legal regulations.

Finally, as far as the effect of uncovered international money flows on the home interest rate level is concerned, it can be stated that it will happen anyway—either in a positive or in a negative direction, either with an increasing or a decreasing tendency. Namely, if the banks—at the behest of their clients—buy foreign currency, then national currency flows to the central bank parallel with the fall in the central bank reserves, and thus the quantity of money in circulation also decreases, which, in turn, influences money market interest rates to rise. On the other hand, when foreign exchange is being sold, the central bank reserves will increase, but, as a counterpart, additional money also gets into circulation, which has a downward effect on interest trends on the money market. Foreign exchange selling is accompanied by money issuing, foreign currency buying, in turn, by money withdrawal, and hence their effect on interests.

It can be stated that interest rate differentials between two equally strong or equally weak currencies can hardly be long-lasting. Such differences are, as a matter of fact, eliminated by the arbitrage activity of the international money market. If, however, one currency is strong while the other is weak, without a near likelihood of change in the parities of a substantial change in the exchange rates, an interest rate differential generally takes shape, since a weak currency is only bought if its interest return is much higher. This is the reason why a weak currency has a greater discount. It is true that this discount does not always and completely reflect the real judgement of the given currency, since central banks—due to psychological reasons—often intervene in respect of discount. It is well known that the Bank of England bought forward significant amounts of pound sterling during the weak period of the pound in order to lessen its discount. The opposite case also occurs quite frequently when central banks exert an influence to raise the interest level (and thus the discount) in order to promote capital inflow.

*

After these preliminary remarks and in order to examine more closely the international money flows themselves and the ways in which the public authorities influence, control and regulate them, we have to make some further general statements.

The first is to repeat what has been said at the beginning of this chapter, namely, that relationship among the individual national money markets concerning their nature, reasons, techniques and consequences are identical with the relationship between a national market and Euromarket. The relations between two national money markets can often be established in practice only through the Euromarket. If, for instance, one has Belgian francs and intends to place them in Austrian schillings for a month, he will first buy dollars with his francs and then purchase the schillings for the simple reason that he will find ample dollars for one month on the market, but will hardly find schillings for one month directly for Belgian francs.

The volume of the Euromarket money flows, as it has been already referred to in the previous chapter, is a multiple of the direct money flows among the national money markets. It is precisely their huge volume that makes the money movements of the Euromarkets so decisively important from the aspect of the foreign exchange and credit policy of the individual countries. Here quantity is transformed into quality.

All the transactions among the national money markets as well as those with the Euromarket are in the hands of the banks. While the number of participants is high in the national—domestic—money markets, it is relatively low in respect of the international ones. The clients are compelled to turn to the banks to make international money transactions, and thus, regardless of who gives the order, the banks conduct the deals. As a consequence, short-term money movements come about under the influence of two factors: one is the opinion of economic circles about some currency, and the other is the banks's foreign exchange policy. These two factors have a mutual effect on each other: often the banks initiate money flows in a certain direction which will later be followed and increased to an unexpected extent by the public.

We are again at the problem of speculation, which is made extremely efficient by the concentrated nature of the market and the high volume of money movements. It is well known that during the crisis of the spring of 1971, before the floating of the DM, there were days when the flow of currency to the Bundesbank reached a billion dollars. These dimensions, as well as the fact that money flows of such size occur in critical periods, indicate that the element of speculation plays a very important role in international money flows. Still, it is not easy to determine where the dividing line is between the rightful endeavour for security and unrightful pure speculation. Many try to find an answer by considering whether owned assets or borrowed money serve as the basis for money flows. According to this view, it is "rightful" to exchange one's own money for foreign currency, to preserve its value, but it is "unrightful" to gain profits through foreign exchange transactions using borrowed money. Many charges are made against multi-national corporations, which, on account of their multi-national character, have the advantage that they can settle foreign exchange transactions within the framework of their own, closed circle, unless there is very rigorous exchange control. Whatever the "moral" judgment might be, it is sure that it is the high liquidity level on the home market, which makes borrowing in national currency easy under favourable conditions, certainly promoting high-scale speculation. This is sufficiently proved by the French events of 1968.

The role of speculative motives in the foreign exchange market crises of recent years is shown also by the history of these troubles recurring at ever shorter intervals. Nobody thinks that these crises are brought about by speculation as nobody can doubt that their cause lies deeper hidden: in the fundamental deficiency of the Bretton Woods monetary system and, last but not least, in the US's monetary policy which disregards its foreign partners' interests, and furthermore, in the unequal economic development of their individual countries participating in the monetary system. Nevertheless, speculation, although not causing these crises, exacerbates them. Therefore, it is not besides the point to give a short summary of the facts.

After some years of relative calm, a series of crises started in the autumn of 1967 with the devaluation of the pound sterling (November 19, 1967). Already in the preceding period as well as afterwards, there was great speculation on the devaluation of the dollar and the revaluation of gold. The central banks of the developed capitalist countries were forced to increase their intervention purchases of dollars; in Paris alone ten tons of gold changed hands at the stock exchange in one day. The year 1968 was marked first of all by the speculation in gold. Starting in January, the gold price steadily rose and in March the London gold stock exchange had to be closed. The one in Paris remained open and within fifteen days more than one billion francs worth of gold changed hands. In the meanime, the gold pool ceased to exist (March 17) and the double gold market was introduced. In May, there was a renewed wave of speculation against the French franc and the pound sterling, which mostly manifested itself on the gold market, and the price of gold went up again. The August 1968 events in Czechoslovakia produced a crisis again which did not calm down entirely, since the devaluation of the franc had already cast its shadow. However, it was devalued only in August 1969, simultaneously with the considerable weakening of the pound sterling. As the revaluation of the Deutsche Mark was foreseeable, speculation was directed not so much at buying gold, but rather DM. This tendency lasted up to a period after the Nixon declaration of August 1971; the bulk of speculation took place not in gold, but on the currency markets. The Deutsche Mark was floating between September 29 and October 24 of 1969, when it was *de jure* revaluated.

The year 1970 passed without any serious crisis; the Canadian dollar started floating in May, but without increasing European speculation. However, the process started already at the end of 1970 and by the beginning of 1971 unfolded to an alarming extent: viz. the massive outflow of dollars towards Europe and mostly towards West Germany. Speculation centred on the possibility of a repeated revaluation of the DM, despite repeated and energetic denials by German monetary authorities and the inflow of currencies into the Federal Republic of Germany rose to an unprecedented extent. On May 9, 1971, the DM was floated again and the Swiss franc and the Austrian schilling were revaluated.

Nevertheless, speculation did not stop. It counted partly on another, possibly major *de jure* revaluation of the Deutsche Mark, and partly on the revaluation of the French franc and the Japanese yen. As a consequence, another inflow of dollars started towards Europe and Japan. At that point came the already mentioned measures of President Nixon. However, these were insufficient to restore tranquility. In December 1971, the dollar's first devaluation by 8 percent, and some other currencies' (especially the DM's and the yen's) revaluation took place. Speculation had anticipated these events well in advance, and by its huge volume had almost forced the affected countries to carry out these changes, i.e., the re- and devaluations. The expected stability was not restored, not even temporarily. Just after these changes in parities, speculation turned to gold, then pressed for the devaluation of the pound sterling which—in order to avoid formal devaluation—was floated in summer 1972.

By the beginning of 1973 it became obvious that the capitalist international monetary system was again in acute crisis. The re-emerging intensified speculative money flows were a clear indication. The USA still strived for solving the new crisis by the revaluation of other countries' currencies. This endeavour, however, was not successful, and the USA was compelled to devalue the dollar again, now by 10 percent. Speculators were well aware of the fact that the dollar's relationship to other important capitalist currencies would change to the detriment of the former, which automatically determined the direction of money flows, namely, an escape from the dollar.

At the same time, the central banks of the capitalist countries had decided to no longer assume the obligation of intervention in favour of the dollar. Thus the dollar became floating in respect to other currencies, which opened further grounds for speculation. From that point on speculation tried to anticipate to what extent central banks would be forced to intervene on behalf of the dollar, despite the cessation of a legal obligation, in order to protect the interests of their own countries. The new changes in parities (the revaluation of the Deutsche Mark twice, followed by the revaluation of the Dutch guilder and the Austrian schilling) again proved right speculative expectations.

Towards the end of 1973, the dollar was clearly gaining in strength. This could be attributed to the fact that the direction of money flows had turned, namely, dollars were bought in great quantities for European currencies and for the yen, partly because the US trade balance improved spectacularly and the improvement of the US balance of payments could also be foreseen, and partly because an unprecedented increase in oil prices affected the more self-sufficient United States much less than the other developed capitalist countries. Speculation based on these facts proved again successful.

At the beginning of 1974, France came into the cross-fire of speculation. It centred on the devaluation of the French franc, based on the anticipation that France could not avoid devaluation as a consequence of the deterioration of her balance of trade and balance of payments due to the rise in oil prices. Finally, the French government was forced to float the commercial franc (the financial franc already had been floating). Soon speculation turned to gold because of rapidly growing rate of inflation on a worldwide scale, and the price of gold rose from the "official" 42.2 dollars an ounce to 180 dollars already by the end of February 1974.

Still, speculation did not calm down. The strong fall in the exchange rate of the Italian lire, as well as the strengthening of the Deutsche Mark, the Swiss franc and the Japanese yen, the series of re- and devaluations within the "European" currency snake and the dropping away of some of the participating countries, were all events in the reasons for which speculation played an important role. The creation of the EMS in 1979 and the narrowing of the fluctuation margins within the EMS did not lessen the speculation either, seeing that medium rates playing the role of the parities in the EMS, may be modified. The reason why such changes have been really effected was—to a large part—speculation recognizing the basic causes and even magnifying them. The same is the situation in respect of the reinforcement of the dollar which started in 1980 and is still lasting as a result of the high interest rate level in the USA. Here, too, speculation amplified the effects stemming from the basic reasons.

All of this proves that speculation uses every chance offered and countermeasures usually fail. In this respect, discussions of a rather theoretical nature took place on whether speculation for devaluation, i.e. a fall in an exchange rate, or revaluation, i.e., a rise in an exchange rate, is more efficient. In principle, it is more effective when it aims for devaluation. This kind of speculation—if it does not get exhausted, that is, if it can continually get a sufficient quantity of the currency in question to the market—will certainly reach its goal, since the reserves of the issuing central bank are limited and once exhausted, the central bank can no longer defend the parity or the exchange rate of its own currency against devaluation or depreciation by further buying. Speculation for revaluation, on the other hand, or for a rise in the exchange rate is not so absolute, since it only throws an obligation upon the issuing central bank of the given currency to buy the inflowing foreign exchange against the national currency and, as a matter of fact, the issuing possibilities of the central banks are much greater than its reserves. And this is the way it is in theory, yet the practical effectiveness of such speculation could be experienced frequently in the recent past, primarily because domestic money issuing also has certain limits (imported inflation).

It was also debated whether the system of almost fixed parities (allowing limited fluctuation) does not promote speculation, since the risk of the speculator is limited. This is true in principle, since if in the system of fixed parities someone uses borrowed money to buy foreign exchange under normal circumstances, he can be sure that by the time of repayment, the buying back of the currency, in which he had been indebted, would not cost him considerably more than the selling price of the given foreign exchange at the time of the purchase. He can also be sure that the exchange rate of the foreign exchange he had bought will not sink considerably below the purchase price. Thus, the system of fixed parities does limit the exchange rate risks to a narrow band between the upper and lower margin—provided there is *no* change in the official parity, i.e., re- or devaluations, in the meantime, which may occur even in the system of fixed parities, in which case the speculator may suffer serious losses. However, this hardly ever occurs in practice, since a speculator is engaged in getting indebted in a currency liable to devaluation and buys currencies liable to be revaluated, and such trends hardly ever reverse themselves within a short period of time. Therefore, the concept concerning the risk-limiting effect of the system of fixed parities is rather theoretical and in fact means that under normal circumstances, when there is no danger of changes in parities, speculation-based losses or profits move within a relatively narrow range. The question arises, of course, whether the greater risk undoubtedly existing in the system of floating—which means not only the possibility of greater losses but also greater profits—does not stimulate rather than moderate willingness to speculate. In recent times many events in connection with the activity and problems of certain banks seem to prove this theory.

These considerations, however, lead to the problems of wider fluctuation limits, to the crawling and free (floating) parities, and as such they do not fall within the scope of our study in the strict sense. Nevertheless, it seems necessary to define these notions exactly, since they often arise in the context of the reform of the international monetary system and since presently—and presumably for a while yet—we live in a world of general floating, where restrictions (e.g. "currency snake" and EMS, respectively) are the exceptions. As far as parities allowing wider fluctuations are concerned, it is well known that the so-called Smithsonian Agreement of the Group of Ten in December 1971 widened the tolerance from the previous ±1 percent to ±2.25 percent. The often mentioned IMF meeting in Jamaica concluded that after the cessation of the present system of floating it wishes to introduce a new general exchange system which would determine the margin of the central exchange rates at $\pm$4.5 percent. As the allowed limits are connected with the range of problems of central bank interventions and, through them, the reserves, their impact on the mechanism of international money flows cannot be underrated.

The concept of "crawling peg" goes far beyond the widening of exchange rate limits since it means an automatic adjustment of official parities. It can be realized by firstly allowing much wider fluctuation margins. When later—let us say in a year—the average rate of exchange of the given currencies will be established within this margin, then for the next period this average will be the official parity around which the exchange rate may again fluctuate between the allowed wider limits. After another period, the new average rate of exchange will become the new official parity, and so on. Therefore, the system of crawling pegs is, in fact, limited—and mostly slowed down—floating.

In the case of free parities, currencies do not have an officially set parity, i.e. the rate of exchange coincides with the parity, thus, the central banks have no intervention obligations and the rate of exchange of the currencies is formed according to the free play of supply and demand (i.e., they float). As mentioned previously, this does not exclude central bank intervention, but it does not bring it on automatically. If a central bank intervenes to defend a floating currency it is called "managed floating", as opposed to "pure floating". Practice, in fact, shows that when the floating of a currency with a formerly fixed parity is decided, it usually serves the temporary concealment of the necessary upward or downward change in parity. Thus floating currencies are floating up- or downward.

It has often been debated whether the fixed parity or the floating system is "better". Perhaps it is not unnecessary to briefly review the arguments. Usually mentioned in the first place among the advantages of floating is that the floating of the national currency makes a freer domestic economic policy possible for the country concerned. It has a freer hand in its budgetary, credit and incomes policy, and is not forced to draw automatically from or to pile up its central bank reserves, since it does not need to defend the parity of its currency. All these theoretically logical advantages, however, can assert themselves only in the case of so-called pure floating, and, as we have seen above, we have not met this phenomenon since the introduction of general floating. On the other hand, hitherto practice cannot serve as a criterion, since during the period of general floating—due to the price explosion of primary raw materials, to recession and to the speeding up of inflation—circumstances were never quite normal.

The only country where the mentioned advantages could really come into their own was the United States, which could carry out a relatively free economic policy at home, hardly taking into consideration the monetary and economic interests of its partners nor the question of the dollar's defence. This, however, can be traced not so much to the freedom stemming from general floating, but rather to the fact that the present monetary system (if there is any) is *de facto* based on the dollar standard; the dollar is a worldwide used money and a means of reserve. It is this fact, together with the economic power of the United States, that makes a more liberal domestic economic policy possible for the USA, and not—or not primarily—the dollar's floating.

As far as the disadvantages of floating are concerned, what is usually mentioned in first place is that floating—especially the general one—leads to a monetary uncertainty which might have a retarding effect on world trade, foreign investments, and thus, on the world economy as a whole. The logic of this criticism cannot be denied, and the present system of general floating undoubtedly involves such a risk. Still, at the same time we must point out that although the capitalist economy has been living in that situation for years, the logically expectable effects cannot yet be stated. The complex examination of the causes of this strange phenomenon would lead us afar, and it is not sure that it would be fruitful. We shall restrict ourselves only to the establishment of facts.

Debate is much more vigorous on the question whether or not

the floating rate system induces inflation. Let us examine some of the arguments attributing an inflationary effect to floating.

It is said that the floating of national currency spurs inflation by increasing import prices. It is a well-known fact that domestic inflation also can be fed by external factors (imported inflation), one of the forms being the increase in the prices of imported goods due to the inflationary rise in the export prices of the partner country. Similar domestic price rises can also be attributed, in respect to imported goods, to a fall in the exchange rate of the buying country's currency. If the buyer's currency is floating, the exchange rate is exposed to more frequent and greater fluctuations than is the case with fixed parities. Domestic prices react immediately to falls in the exchange rate, while they react much more slowly and to a smaller extent to rises in the exchange rate and that is why floating the currency has an inflationary effect.

According to another argument, floating a currency induces inflation through costs. The essence of this reasoning is that while in the case of fixed parities the greater share of the exchange rate risk is taken by the central bank due to its intervention obligation, in the case of floating this risk is completely taken by the economic units, which, including it in their prices, raise the price level, thus further contributing to inflation. The next argumentation seemsmore weighty: it relies on the fact that the frequent and great exchange fluctuations which follow in the wake of floating increase the banks' and the economic units' preference for liquidity. This is disadvantageous in two respects: partly because the short-term Euromarket—which is the breeding ground for speculation, increasing instability—grows further in volume, and partly because, due to increased effort at liquidity, the habit to finance medium-and long-term credits from short-term sources grows stronger, endangering security. (This is called maturity transformation.)

Incidentally, those consequences of floating that are considered advantageous are often disputed by the defenders of fixed parities, who call attention to negative phenomena arising from them.

Thus, starting from the two premises, namely, that floating makes a less restrictive domestic economic policy possible (the relativeness of this we have seen above) and that inflation involves a permanent redistribution in conformity with real social forces, they arrive at the conslusion that in the case of floating, wages and profits are freed more readily, which, in turn, leads to the further growth of inflation. Whatever the truth of these premises might be, it is certain that floating at least does not impede the freeing of wages and profits.

The opponents of floating often mention that general floating is an unfair monetary system, since the United States makes a unilateral profit on it. Undoubtedly, the burden of intervention is hardly borne by the USA, while the other participants, for different reasons, are compelled to intervene massively, even in the case of floating currencies. It is also true, however, that in the Bretton Woods monetary system of fixed parities the FED *de jure* was not obliged to intervene and did not do so *de facto* either. But the survival of this privilege even after the collapse of the system is not caused—as we have seen—by general floating, but by the still existing dominant role of the dollar. While this situation prevails also in the system of floating, it is indeed not urgent for the United States to put an end to it.

It would be rather useless to continue to follow the arguments of the supporters and opponents of floating, all the more because both refer mostly to the theoretical case of pure floating. Anyway, it is certain that general floating could not produce the expected effect in practice, i.e., a significant promotion of balance-of-payments equalization. Perhaps it can be traced back to those abnormal circumstances under which the world economy has been operating since the introduction of general floating, but it is certain that floating was insufficient to remedy these circumstances.

*

When we shall speak about influencing, controlling and regulating short-term money flows, the first factor to be stressed will be that these measures always suppose and mean central (i.e., central bank) and, finally, state intervention. State intervention exists in the case of both free and restricted foreign exchange systems, the difference being only in degree, in its particular or general character.

Let us first see what measures are at the disposal of the central state authorities to influence and control short-term international money flows under a free foreign exchange system. All the measures discussed below have been used by central banks in recent years.

The first such measure—one already mentioned in several other connections—is direct central bank intervention on the foreign exchange market, which the central banks were under obligation to execute, according to the rules of the Bretton Woods monetary system, as soon as their currencies reached the intervention level. But central banks often intervene even when not so obliged, in order to influence the exchange rate between the intervention points, and perhaps also when the national currency is floating—as mentioned before. The means of intervention is buying (thus raising exchange rates) or selling (with the opposite effect). Central banks can intervene indirectly, too, by lending a given currency cheap or dear since one of the causes generating the international money flows lies in the interest rate differentials. A direct central bank intervention through the buying or selling of a currency appears in the form of cash of forward deals. The latter has the advantages of a time shift concerning the fall in central bank reserves as a consequence of the selling of foreign exchange and concerning domestic money issue against foreign exchange as a consequence of its purchase. This time shift is often desirable. For instance, the Bundesbank, in order to prevent a too high premium on the floating DM against the dollar, effected intervention purchases of dollars with Deutsche Marks, and it often did it in the form of a forward deal lest it would boost the economy by issuing Marks at the time of intervention, considered especially inappropriate from this aspect. There are cases when the central bank intervenes to bring about the higher exchange rates of foreign exchange expressed in the national currency in order to diminish the number of potential buyers of foreign exchange. This is what the Italian central bank did during the revaluation crisis of the Deutsche Mark when it drove the dollar exchange rate of the lire up to the upper intervention point—previously it was around the low mark—in order to decrease the possibility of buying DM for cheap dollars.

Central bank credit policy is also an often used means of altering international money flows. We have already pointed out the interconnections between uncovered money flows and domestic interest rate levels, from the aspect of international money flows. It is obvious that these interconnections may also be used from the interest level side to influence international money flows. We have also mentioned that an ample domestic money supply extends the possibilities and means of speculation directed at the devaluation or the depreciation of the currency of the given country. Evidently, credit policy, the aim of which is to influence and control the interest level and money supply and thereby to affect primarily the domestic business cycle, can simultaneously be an effective tool for altering uncovered international money flows, sometimes to such an extent that it even becomes a primary goal, and certain credit policy measures are introduced in order to influence the inflow or outflow of money.

The detailed review of the measures included in credit policy goes beyond the scope of this study. Nevertheless, it is perhaps worthwhile to mention that central banks have a wide range of possible courses in this field. The most important means with which the central bank can influence the interest level differ from country to country. In the Anglo-Saxon world it is chiefly the open market operations, i.e., intervention on the short-term credit markets. In France, it is primarily the appropriate adjustment and fixing of the rediscount rate. (It should be noted that the Banque de France has heavily intervened on the open market in the recent past and adopted other credit policy measures as well, diminishing the importance of the rediscount rate.) In order to indicate how much the fixing of the rediscount rate has been employed in France to alter international money flows either to defend the franc or to avoid money inflows, we list here the changes of the French rediscount rate in the decade between 1967 and 1977:

First half of 1967	3.5 percent
July 3, 1967	5.0 percent
November 12, 1968	6.0 percent
July 13, 1969	7.0 percent
October 8, 1969	8.0 percent
August 27, 1970	7.5 percent
October 20, 1970	7.0 percent
January 8, 1971	6.5 percent
May 13, 1971	6.75 percent
October 28, 1971	6.5 percent
January 12, 1972	6.0 percent
April 6, 1972	5.75 percent
November 2, 1972	6.5 percent
December 1, 1972	7.5 percent
July 5, 1973	8.5 percent
August 2, 1973	9.5 percent
September 20, 1973	11.0 percent
June 20, 1974	13.0 percent
January 9, 1975	12.0 percent
February 27, 1975	11.0 percent
April 10, 1975	10.0 percent
June 5, 1975	9.5 percent
September 4, 1975	8.0 percent
July 22, 1976	9.5 percent
September 23, 1976	10.5 percent
August 31, 1977	9.5 percent

Comparing the imaginary curve of the rediscount rate with that of the changes in the international monetary situation, one can observe many analogies. Before the events of 1968, France, in fact, carried out a policy by wich she was able to hold the domestic interest level somewhat above that of the Eurodollar through the cautious manipulation of the rediscount rate, thus preventing capital outflow. After the shock to the franc, France was forced to adopt more drastic measures in order to make placements in francs more desirable for foreign capital through the interest rate. When the capital inflow turned dangerous, she cut the interest level, but the franc's position was gradually weakening, she raised it more and more.

The fact that the curves do not completely coincide is due to two factors. The first is that influencing the interest level is not only a monetary policy measure, but an economic one as well, and their respective considerations do not always agree. (High interest attracts capital, but lowering the interest level may give too great an impetus to business activity. On the other hand, low interest may cause capital outflow, but raising it may endanger economic prosperity.) Economic interconnections are manifold—high interests affect the price level, too—and every measure may bring about a variety of consequences, and therefore they should be employed cautiously and never to their fullest extent.

The other reason why the French rediscount rate did not follow closely the international monetary situation is that there are a lot of other means of influencing interest level and money supply in the credit policy arsenal. The most drasic among them is the quantitative restriction of loans. This was also applied in France and very strictly, too, and at different periods. There are other quantitative restrictions which affect the interest level rather than the credit volume. Such is the control of the rediscount ceiling—the volume which can be given by the banks to the central bank for rediscounting—and the means of obligatory reserves. The latter means that the banks have to put a deposit not bearing an interest return at the central bank after their deposits and perhaps after their loans, too. This certainly makes credit more expensive and, to a certain degree, may also affect the global volume of lending. In order to achieve a given credit policy aim, the above-mentioned measures can be applied either simultaneously or in well-planned segments.

Another frequently applied measure—not of credit policy origin—by the central bank is the adequate influencing of the activities of domestic banks on foreign money markets, primarily the Euromarkets. We have seen that certain money movements assert themselves in the shift between the central bank's reserves and the banks' foreign exchange stock. In order to counteract that, it seems obvious that the central banks need to influence commercial banks so as to make them recover their outstanding foreign exchange claims and turn over the "repatriated" foreign exchange to the central banks for national currency. This is what happened in the Italian case mentioned in Chapter II, when Italy's central bank obtained foreign exchange this way, on the one hand, and made the domestic market liquid with the lires paid out against foreign currencies, which was in line with its credit policy objectives, on the other.

An opposite tendency may be observed, too, in that the central bank can stimulate the banks' foreign exchange lendings. This is well illustrated by the example of the Bundesbank (also mentioned in Chapter II). For a lengthy period this central bank put at the German banks' disposal the inflowed dollars so that the banks could place them on the Euromarket; in fact, with the help of swap deals, it even protected the banks from the risk of a possible interim revaluation of the Deutsche Mark. It did so partly because it did not want to increase its dollar reserves and partly because it wanted to avoid having the exchange of Eurodollars into DM—which decreases the Euromarket supply—raise the interest rates on the Eurodollar market.

The Bundesbank was compelled eventually to stop these stimulating interventions, because the Eurodollar placements of the German banks were used for further Deutsche Mark purchases, and thus the dollars changed against Marks and flowed again to the Bundesbank. This was when the German central bank made the other German banks buy US Treasury bills with the dollars it had put at their disposal. The disadvantage of this action was, in turn, that it decreased the dollar supply of the Euromarket, and finally the Bundesbank stopped swap credits to the German banks, no longer guaranteeing protection against the increasingly serious risk of the revaluation of the Deutsche Mark.

The restrictive regulation concerning non-residents' bank accounts in national currency is a further way of influencing short-term international capital movements. This can take various forms. Between 1963 and 1966 and later, at the time of the massive capital inflow in December 1971, it was forbidden again in France that banks should pay interest on money placed in the franc accounts of non-residents. This measure was taken in order to avoid a capital inflow, thus, imported inflation. A similar practice was the introduction of a negative interest in Switzerland, which required that new foreign clients pay interest on their deposits at Swiss banks.

These steps could be effective only to a certain degree, since such regulations can easily be by-passed. This also goes for the German regulation, which stipulated that banks establish at the central bank reserves *(Bardepot)* of 100 percent after deposits by non-residents, which, of course, decreased the interest paid on them.

We may mention here the most usual way of by-passing such regulations. If a foreign bank deposits at a domestic bank a sum in domestic currency on which the domestic bank is not allowed to pay interest, the operation will be presented as a swap loan. It will be demonstrated that actually the deposit is not really a deposit but the part paid in home currency of such a swap, the counterpart of which is a loan granted by the domestic bank to a foreign partner in foreign exchange. The amount of the foreign exchange part of the swap will be deposited by the foreign bank as a foreign exchange deposit at the domestic bank, i.e., the amount in question is in fact given back to the domestic bank. Thus the original situation is restored since the amount of the deposit in domestic currency has not changed and the amount of foreign exchange coming from the other part of the swap loan has been returned to the domestic bank. Given that there are no regulations forbidding the payment of the expenses of a swap deal to the foreign partner, nor the payment of interest on deposits in foreign exchange, the domestic bank will settle with its foreign partner the question of interest this way, paying what it would have paid after the deposit in domestic currency in the first place had there been no regulations to the contrary.

There is another, more complicated measure designed precisely to encourage money inflow; it was applied by the Bank of England, and not entirely without success. The main point of it was that, besides maintaining a high domestic interest rate level, the British central bank provided through forward deals a possibility for foreign sterling depositors to exchange cheaply their pound-sterlings into another currency. Thus, though no new money inflows towards England were created this way, neither did the money already placed there leave as depositors felt secure with such a guarantee. This slowed the rhythm of the fall of reserves at the Bank of England, since even if foreign depositors made use of this possibility, they did not do so immediately. However, in this case it was undoubtedly the Bank of England with the lion's share of the currency risk of devaluation of the pound sterling, which is a double-edged weapon.

All of these measures applied to influence or regulate uncovered short-term money flows bring only moderate results. They give the central banks a temporary opportunity to direct, retard or promote these money flows somewhat, but the obstacles they pose are weak. Under normal circumstances, they may slow down the flow but cannot resist the flood.

Therefore, and in the interest of defending the international monetary system and in the spirit of mutual assistance, there have been international attemps to influence and direct the discussed money flows. One of these international measures is the swap loans granted by central banks to those central banks whose currencies are in danger. The nature of these swaps has been already examined. While still in force, the gold pool served also to ensure relative tranquillity on the international money markets by limiting speculation in gold. The gold pool was established in August 1961. Its participants were the United States (up to 50 percent), the United Kingdom, Belgium, France, The Netherlands, the Federal Republic of Germany, Italy, and Switzerland. France—without formally leaving the gold pool—ceased participating in it as of June 1967. This move was in line with the concept of the well-known late economist, J. Rueff, and which was introduced by President de Gaulle, according to which France's external economic policy should strive for more independence vis-à-vis the US, and consequently she had opposed the gold-exchange standard and the dollar's increasing dominance, wanting instead to designate gold as the basis of the international monetary system, considering its revaluation desirable.

The aim of the gold pool was to allow intervention on the gold market whenever necessary in order not to let the gold price substantially exceed the official parity. The pool's intervention sales (and later also purchases) were carried out through the bank of England. The participants established joint reserves and in certain periods even earned profits which were divided among themselves according to their respective shares, as were the losses which were rather more frequent. The pool was dissolved in March 1968 during the gold crisis because the participants realized that they did not want to—nor could they afford to—intervene on the massive scale that would have been required. It was then that the two-tier gold market was established and the USA declared that it will convert gold at the official parity only for central banks. Under such circumstances, with the dollar's full convertibility terminated, the gold pool was no longer needed since its purpose was to protect the central bank gold reserves of the United States and to avoid the dollar's devaluation against gold, the necessity for which already appeared at that time.

In connection with the supranational means serving, to some extent, the control and restriction of the international money movements, mention should be made of the FECOM (Fond Européen du Coopération Monétaire) functioning within the framework of the EMS which may be considered as the core of the common bank of the EEC, yet to be established. As a regional organization, it aims at keeping within tolerable limits the fluctuation of the currencies of the countries participating in the EMS, in a way that the necessary means are put at the disposal of the central banks for intervention purposes. In the long-run, it is intended for this organization to undertake the intervention activity of the individual central banks and to perform it in the interest of the common EEC currency's, the ECU's stability.

A further measure, applied often and to a great extent, is the recycling of outflown money. This means that those central banks which are beneficiaries of inflows, or, at least, not its victims, lend money to those central banks which are in difficulty as a consequence of money outflow, in order to ease their situation and to enable them to avoid restrictive measures.

The most important case of international assistance was perhaps the international guarantee of the sterling balances. The countries belonging to the sterling-belt have significant pound sterling claims against Great Britain, and these are called sterling balances. In 1969, Britain guaranteed that in certain conditions it was prepared to repay these claims in dollars. This guarantee, however, was based on the reciprocal assurance given to Britain by the pool of the central banks under the authority of the BIS.

Any joint assistance on an international scale by central banks is, however, only temporary since the loans granted as aid in various forms must be repaid sooner or later (and rather the former). Though it is true that the SDR introduced by the IMF will presumably play a gradually increasing role in central bank reserves and therefore will be employable for intervention purposes within the limits mentioned in Chapter II, but their volume is rather low for the time being, and their usability in this respect is yet to be tested by a major crisis on the foreign exchange markets.

In examining the possibilities of influencing long-term capital movements (still under the conditions of a free foreign exchange system), we have to point out again that, in respect of their effects, they are similar to uncovered short-term international money flows as they usually have no covering counter-parts. Consequently, these capital flows directly affect the central banks' reserves and domestic liquidity. This is why they are often subject to special regulations. It is easy to understand that administrative regulations are more exact and more numerous concerning capital exports than in the case of capital imports. Still, there are examples for the latter, too. For instance, in 1965 a special tax was imposed in West Germany on the coupons of German bonds held by non-residents. In France, a regulation dated from 1967 (i.e., in a period when there was no exchange control) obliged foreigners to register their investments on French territory and gave a delaying force to the authorities' declarations albeit for economic rather than monetary purposes.

Restrictions concerning capital exports are frequent in the case of both foreign bond issues and direct foreign investments. Already before the repeated crises of the Bretton Woods monetary system there was hardly a country (except the United States and the Federal Republic of Germany) where there was not a "waiting list" for long-term foreign bond issues, which list, by inserting intervals, delayed and restricted these issues. The most effective means of restricting capital exports, are, however, the taxation measures which are often adopted by governments. The Interest Equalization Tax adopted by the United States in 1963 was among these measures.

After reviewing the measures aimed at influencing international money and capital movements under the circumstances of the free exchange system, let us examine what exchange control means in this respect. It undoubtedly means increased restrictions. In the case of exchange control there is generally greater distinction made between residents and non-residents, and the restrictions are usually more severe in the case of the former, especially—although, as we shall see, not exclusively—if the transactions in question would worsen the country's external monetary position. These restrictions, which close up money markets, quite often divert money flows into illegal channels and give rise to parallel—black market—exchange rates.

The reason for introducing exchange controls is the increasing need to defend against uncovered international money flows. This need usually arises with the aim of preventing money outflow, but it may also have the opposite purpose—to prevent money inflow. One of the main objectives in establishing the Bretton Woods international monetary system was precisely to gradually lift restrictions in the member countries—especially in the developed European capitalist countries, where, as a remnant of the Second World War, exchange control was still in force—and, after the general liberalization of trade, to largely set free money movements, too. This was gradually realized. Although, as we have seen above, there are some restrictions even under the so-called free exchange system, and the point whether a country's exchange system is "free" or "controlled" is merely a matter of degree, still, one can say that by 1967 (fairly late, since France had lifted certain restrictions only then) the majority of the most important IMF member countries and all of the developed capitalist countries had an unrestricted foreign exchange system concerning money and capital movements as well.

As the monetary crises became increasingly frequent (devaluation of the pound sterling, the shock to the French franc in the summer of 1968) the restrictions became more numerous and severe, and France—though other countries with threatened currencies also made use of innumerable exchange restrictions—was compelled to admit the need to control and regulate the international money flows, i.e., to introduce exchange control. It would lead us afar and it is not the topic of our study to examine the part played in this decision by French political philosophy which tends towards a state-directed economy and how this had clashed with German neo-liberalism, which, of course, was later forced to make concessions in this respect. Here it is sufficient to state that exchange control in France had to be introduced in order to prevent an escape from the franc, the money outflow.

It is a strange turn of economic fate that the regulations concerning exchange control brought about for the above reasons, were also suitable in the second half of 1971 but for an opposite purpose, i.e. to check money inflow, of course together with the introduction of a double exchange market and other supplementary measures. As to these supplementary measures, we have to note that they were drastic and the franc's convertibility was temporarily suspended even in respect to non-residents and non-residents' francs were, at least partly, frozen, and thus the possibility of their domestic use was also restricted.

It is interesting by the way that the French exchange control has survived in many respects the franc's floating, although the notion of floating would, as a matter of fact, exclude exchange control, the regulations of which are intended precisely to limit the theoretical freedom of floating. In practice, in cases of monetary danger the states and their central banks—even if their currency is floating—adopt a number of measures actually belonging to the domain of exchange control. This proves that the "free" and the "controlled" foreign exchange systems differ only in degree but not in kind.

The technical measures which transfer long-term capital flows to a closed market separated from the general money market by measures of the authorities, can also be included in the concept of exchange control. This was in fact the situation in connection with the French so-called *devise titre*. This definition meant that a resident could buy foreign securities by using only such foreign exchange which originated from the sale of some foreign securities, having been owned by a resident, against foreign exchange. These foreign exchanges, called *devise titre*, participated in the market transactions, but their occurrence being relatively rare and the demand therein sometimes rather keen, they could be purchased only at a considerably high premium. This premium often served as an index of the black market rate of the French franc. In 1971, the *devise titre* was abolished. A further example for this delimination was the so-called dollar investment market which functioned for a long time in Britain. Apart from certain especially profitable foreign investments, foreign exchange for the purpose of foreign investment could be bought only on this market. The market was supplied by 75 percent of the foreign exchange coming from the liquidation of foreign investments—not too abundantly as a matter of fact—so that sometimes a 50 percent premium had to be paid on foreign exchange obtained on this market. The Belgian "free market" was also a market for long-term financial transactions, although certain short-term deals were also transacted here. The Belgian free market "financial" franc also quite often showed a certain discount which, in turn, reduced capital outflow, thus making long-term capital placements in Belgium more profitable.

It is disputable whether the technical measures mentioned earlier (which, besides, according to Chapter VIII of the Articles of Agreement of the IMF, may be applied only with the approval of the IMF) are by all means part of an exchange control system, since in Belgium or in Britain, when the financial franc or the dollar investment pound was established, there was no exchange control in the true sense of the word. Yet, it is beyond that these measures are aimed at restricting capital flows, that they mean state interference in their freedom and, at least in respect of long-term international capital flows, an increasing tightening. Therefore, I believe, they had to be reviewed logically in this context.

It is, however, incontestable that the global and consistent introduction of the double exchange rate—executed by France after the suspension of the dollar's convertibility by President Nixon in August 1971—belongs to the field of exchange control, even if its aim was not protection against money outflow, but money inflow, i.e., imported inflation. Its relatively smooth realization was attained through the mechanism and official machinery of the exchange control that had been introduced much earlier.

Already in the summer of 1971, the money inflow to France—due to an expected devaluation of the dollar and revaluation of the franc—assumed proportions that seriously troubled the French government. In order to maintain the otherwise unstable export competitiveness of French industries and thereby the level of employment and economic activity, the government wanted to avoid having to introduce revaluation, the most efficient tool against money inflow. For the same reason, it did not want to float the franc either, which, in the given circumstances, would have been equal to the franc's *de facto* revaluation. Therefore, when France was compelled to move as a consequence of the Nixon regulations, the government chose a third alternative: the introduction of the double exchange rate, the double foreign exchange market.

The basic idea behind this is that payments originating from the strictly commercial export–import turnover should be separated from all other, non-commercial international money flows. The purchases and sales of foreign exchange related to the former took place on the "official" commercial market, while any other exchange was effected on the so-called "financial market". The exchange rate of the commercial franc to be exchanged on the official market against the dollar and other currencies remained at the earlier official parity and the central bank continued intervening between the margins determined by the IMF rules in favour of the dollar on the market of the commercial franc until the dollar became floating in February 1973. Thus, the commercial franc—just like the franc before it—had remained tied in the old way to the dollar and later to the European currencies commonly floating against the dollar. On the other hand, the floating financial franc's rate changed according to the free play of supply and demand, as much as it was possible under the circumstances of exchange control, since on the market of the financial franc the central bank did not intervene—at least not in principle—as it was not obliged to do so.

The double market, the practical employment of which undoubtedly entails many disadvantages and even more difficulties, was, in fact, suitable as it did not reduce export competitiveness (indeed, as a consequence of the *de jure* or *de facto* revaluations in the partner countries, even increased it), while restraining imports by making them more expensive, and primarily because it prevented the money inflow against which France was then wishing to protect herself.

Still, it must be mentioned that the regulation—which we will return to later—could not completely keep away money inflows based on speculation on the franc's revaluation. As a matter of fact, any non-resident could buy commercial francs (the cheap franc) for foreign exchange. It is true that the use of these commercial francs was rather limited, but if their holder kept them in an account in France, speculation on the franc's revaluation, when it occurred and depending on the extent, might have been profitable, unless the interest losses (these accounts were not interest bearing) had cancelled out the profits. As with any speculation, two factors might have played a role here: the likely extent of parity change and the difference in interest. As the French government intended to revaluate the franc only to a slight extent and as the date of the monetary settlement could not be foreseen for a long time, the French government did not consider the abovementioned speculation dangerous, and therefore it did not exclude its possibility. When the date of the settlement seemed to approach (in December 1971) and events showed that this gamble had been risked by many people, new restrictive regulations were introduced (freezing, turning non-residents' franc claims inconvertible, further restriction of their use especially in respect to more recently inflowed francs). These supplementary measures were later abolished together with other especially rigid ones as a consequence of the monetary settlement at the end of 1971, but the system of the double exchange market, just like exchange control, remained in force for the time being. It is interesting that the French government continued to maintain the double foreign exchange market for a short time even when it also floated the commercial franc in 1974. Its abolishment two months later was explained by the fact that the deficit of the commercial-franc balance due to oil-price rises and the surplus of the financial-franc balance due to public borrowing would have both become too big if the system of separation had been maintained.

The success of the whole system depended on the consistent execution of separation between the commercial and the financial markets, though the delimitation did not prove easy, neither in principle nor in time. In principle, the intention was to make the financial market the general, and the commercial market the exceptional one, the latter serving strictly for export and import transactions. Thus, the contervalue of intellectual export–import (like engineering), foreign exchange from transit deals, etc. were transferred to the financial market. The rules regarding the time factor were so rigid that the foreign exchange countervalue of the exported goods—if it came in before becoming due—had to be sold on the financial market where the exporter received, for a time, fewer francs for his foreign exchange than on the commercial market, where he could have gone had the money arrived after being due. All this was done in order to reduce foreign exchange inflow as much as possible. For the same reason even banks were forbidden for a time to take credits in foreign exchange.

Measures concerning the double market were also extremely strict concerning non-residents. Non-residents could possess two kinds of franc accounts: foreign accounts in commercial or in financial francs. As mentioned earlier, claims on commercial accounts could be used only for the settling goods imports, but the usability of claims in financial francs was also limited. It should be recalled here that the financial franc was considered foreign exchange and as a result if a non-resident wanted to meet an obligation which—according to regulations—ought to have been paid in financial francs drawn from his commercial franc account, he then had to purchase financial francs for his commercial ones in the form of a foreign exchange transaction—but even this was not always possible.

Obviously, this called for a very complicated control-system and a sizable administration, the maintenance of which was up to the banks. The complicated and artificial nature of the system unavoidably led to anomalies, to unforeseen, unwanted and even harmful consequences, just like exchange control in general, of which the system of the double foreign exchange market is an especially sharp and qualified form. A very characteristic example of such an anomaly was when the French banks were not allowed to borrow foreign currency from abroad, but were allowed to effect such credit transactions with residents, i.e., with other domestic banks, a real, parallel, and internal inter-bank Eurodollar credit market came into being in France, with much higher interest rates than those found on the external Eurodollar credit market.

As a matter of fact, despite its faults, insufficiencies and lack of justness, the Bretton Woods monetary system had a logic of its own, reflecting the power relations existing at the time of its establishment. The stricter the limitations, the less were they compatible with this logic, and therefore they led to greater and greater anomalies, and, finally, to the collapse of the system.

To sum up, we can state again that among international money and capital flows the uncovered ones are those that are really interesting from our viewpoint, since only they affect the quantity of central bank reserves, the balance of payments, exchange rates, liquidity, and the domestic interest level. Under quiet circumstances—using the word "normal" would show perhaps exaggerated optimism—these uncovered money flows are induced by interest level differences; in critical periods, however, they lose their efficacy. The measures adopted in order to influence these money flows in the desirable direction are not entirely successful, and the introduction of exchange control is partly a double-edged and partly not an absolutely sure remedy. Still, just because of the huge volume of these money flows, developed capitalist countries endeavour to ensure some influence on these flows even if they do not introduce an exchange control. There is no country where the state does not wish to influence uncovered money flows by some credit policy or other measures, or which exhibits a completely neutral attitude towards them. It is only a question of degree what steps the individual states take and how far they go in applying them.

Much was said in this chapter about the speculative character of money flows, or about money flows induced by speculation. It would be a mistake, however, to draw the conclusion that money flows of great importance and a definite (unilateral) direction can be traced to speculation exclusively. These money flows have a fundamental economic basis which is recognized and gambled on by speculation, thus increasing their impact. Let us refer again, for an example, to the speculative money flows in connection with the French franc's devaluation and the Deutsche Mark's revaluation, i.e., the two-way shift of the two currencies' parity and all the more since shifts in this direction occurred frequently. Here the main cause lay in the opposite shift of price levels and the purchasing power of the currencies of the two neighbouring countries which have a huge volume of mutual trade turnover and which are in competition for many third markets. This basic situation was recognized by speculation, drawing—correctly—the conclusion that if anything "happens" to these currencies, it will be only in the known direction. At the same time, speculation undoubtedly contributed to the situation that "something really should happen", first to the franc and later to the DM, partly by directing public attention to the real situation of these currencies and partly by contributing to the intensity of the money flows naturally resulting from the given situation.

Chapter V

The Interconnections between the External Monetary Position and Domestic Liquidity

Many references have been made so far to the fact that there must be some interconnections between a country's external monetary position, changes in the balance of payments, central bank reserves, and domestic liquidity. The central bank issues domestic currency against inflowed foreign exchange, which may lead to a certain form of imported inflation or may be one of its causes, and when the purchase of foreign exchange takes place at the central bank, it is done against domestic currency, with the amount coming to the central bank being withdrawn from circulation. Thus, the foreign exchange purchases of the central bank increase, while its sales decrease domestic liquidity in the case of uncovered money flows. This is the interconnection between the foreign exchange position and central bank reserves, on the one hand, and domestic liquidity, on the other. As far as the interconnection between the other element of a country's monetary position—i.e., the balance between foreign short-term claims and obligations in national currency, on the one hand, and domestic liquidity, on the other—is concerned, this is of the same direction but more direct, since if this balance tends to be active, it involves an increase of liquidity in domestic currency, while if it tends to be passive, then it involves the latter's decrease.

We shall also deal with the interconnections between *foreign exchange position* and domestic liquidity, since from the aspect of the external monetary position, foreign exchange claims and liabilities are much more significant than those in national currency. This is all the more so as international money and capital movements—the effects of which are the subject of this study—are realized in the foreign exchange sector, since we can speak about international money flows—in line with our previous definition—if foreign exchange conversion takes place. For the sake of precision, let us note that by the term "liquidity" we mean the totality of monetary and quasi-monetary assets. The means of payments in circulation, thus money (notes and coins), are of monetary character, while by quasi-monetary we mean immediately mobilizable deposits at sight or short-term, as well as Treasury bills, etc.

Having outlined the logical interconnections, let us see how these things evolve. The facts show that the liquidities trend has a remarkable regularity; if we present the figures of some consecutive years in a graphical form, the curves are almost the same. This is also true for longer periods. In France, for instance, from 1959 to 1969 and even to 1970, the growth rate of liquidity was about the same, around 10 percent annually, although in the given period a lot of things happened in respect of the French economy and currency: devaluations and stabilization periods alternated and France's foreign exchange position reversed itself many times.

Looking even farther into the past, one can make a similar statement concerning money supply in a narrow sense. Its growth rate between 1885 and 1914 in France was about 3 percent annually. World War I meant a break in this respect: the quantity of money in circulation grew suddenly and the continuously increasing amount of credits granted to the Treasury speeded up the rate of growth significantly. World War II had the same effect on money supply, i.e., on its growth rate, again by the "advances" granted to the Treasury. Apart from wartimes, the growth rate in the different historical periods was fairly similar. From the data of other West-European countries between 1951 and 1969, one may draw the conclusion that the coefficient of the money supply growth showed, in general, remarkable stability and was not really sensitive to the changes in the given countries' foreign exchange position.

If the former logical statement concerning the interrelation between foreign exchange position and domestic liquidity and the empirical statement concerning the development of domestic liquidity are equally true, then the contradiction can only be solved by supposing that other factors influencing domestic liquidity and the development of the foreign exchange position in general somehow compensate each other, namely, the increasing or decreasing effect of the foreign exchange position on domestic liquidity is neutralized by another factor exerting a simultaneous opposite influence. Liquidity is created by money emission. The issuing activity is carried out by the banking system, including the central bank. The central bank issues money against gold and foreign exchange, as well as against credits granted to the state; the commercial banks of the banking system issue against credits granted to other debtors in national currency since in developed capitalist countries the central banks do not grant loans directly except to the state, aside from a few exceptional cases. From our point of view, however, this differentiation is of no interest since the central bank refinances the bulk of the other banks' issuing activity and, as a directing organ of credit policy, regulates it as well, and thus emission depends, in the end, on the central bank: directly against gold and foreign exchange, indirectly against credit-granting. Since issues can only be effected if based on these sources, and the foreign exchange position, as we have seen, has hardly any influence on liquidity (though theoretically it should), the supposition is obvious that the counteracting element is the tendency of the credit volume.

The Banque de France, wishing to defend herself against the accusations made in connection with her credit policy during the franc-crisis of 1968, made a careful statistical examination concerning the interdependence between liquidity, on the one hand, and, on the other, the credits granted to the economy, claims against the Treasury, central bank reserves—as the most essential elements of the foreign exchange position—and the net foreign claims, both in relation to France and to other West-European countries. The essence of the mentioned accusations was that the French central bank, in order to boost the economy and production which slowed as a consequence of the near revolution of May 1968, pumped an additional credit of about 3 billion francs into economy, lifted rediscount ceilings and thus promoted the outflow "national" capital, an escape from the franc. The result of the analysis seems to prove the verity of these accusations because, as a consequence of accessory credits, the level of domestic liquidity increased only for a short period and thus the supposition is evident that outflow was the counter-item of growth. Theoretically, concerning the level of liquidity, analyses proved the necessity of additional lending, since they came to the conclusion that when the foreign exchange position suddenly reverses itself (e.g. when surplus becomes a deficit), it does not generally entail a parallel change in liquidity. The global sum of money in circulation and quasi-monetary means is generally indifferent to the individual changes in the different sources of money emission. We can suppose that the economy of a country always needs a certain amount of liquidity and this necessity is independent of the sources of liquidity. In other words, when a source is exhausted, another has to be opened wider in order to ensure the liquidity level required by the economy. This, in itself, seems to support the idea of compensation, but fails to settle the concrete dispute since it does not answer the question whether the growing money outflow was the cause or the consequence of the accessory credits.

The idea of compensation is also supported, at least to a certain degree, by other Banque de France data concerning earlier periods, thus not related to the problems of the present financial policy, but rather dealing with the development of the counterparts of the credit volume. The data reveal that in certain periods, such as the 1830's, around 1850 and after 1870, the growth of the central bank gold holdings coincided in France with a strong decrease of credits granted to the economy. Such interconnections of a compensatory nature can be demonstrated also in the calm period of 1885—1914. On the other hand, during the war, when lending to the Treasury became the preponderant source of issuing, the increase of this source was not compensated by a decrease at other sources. Compensation cannot be shown for the period 1959—1967 either, as the increase of central bank reserves was not accompanied by a drop in the borrowing activity of the economy.

As for the data of other West-European countries which were also presented by the Banque de France for the period 1959—1969, it seems unnecessary to give the concrete figures here. In the cases of West-Germany and Italy, they do not show a trend from which any kind of compensation might be supposed. In respect of Belgium and The Netherlands, however, one can conclude that between the net foreign claims and the total amount of credit granted to the economy, there is an opposite relationship.

These statistics suggest that there really are certain interconnections of a compensatory nature between the amount of credit granted to the economy and to the Treasury and the development of the foreign exchange position, at least under certain circumstances—nor is this generally disputed by economic experts. However, the statistics do not answer many other questions that are important from our viewpoint. These questions are the following: Does this relationship really exist (and if it does, how come it cannot be shown by the examples of France, Germany and Italy)? How far is it a result of automatic or of purposeful interference? What are the laws regulating them and the causes which might neutralize them? Do the credits granted to the Treasury and to the economy have the same role? And last but not least, does the interdependence assert itself regardless of the source of the impulse (i.e., either from the credits side or from the foreign exchange position side). These problems are the subjects of fundamental theoretical debates.

While delving into the details of these debates would lead too far from our topic, we do need to examine a little closer what the effects of the changes in the foreign exchange position are in practice in domestic liquidity, and how the central banks—due to the recognized effects—react in their credit policy to the changes in the foreign exchange position trends, and in the balance of payments. The fact of this reaction in itself indicates that the central banks accept some form of the interdependence as a basis of action but their purely practical regulations should not be interpreted as the taking of sides in the debate on the nature and laws of interdependence.

*

Let us see in practice the effect of the development of the foreign exchange position on domestic liquidity, both when its balance is active and when it is passive, differentiating in both cases between bank liquidity and the liquidity of economic units. If the foreign exchange balance is active, the banks obtain money for the foreign currency sold to the central bank, thus repaying their debts there. Consequently, the amount of gold and foreign exchange increases on the central bank's balance sheet, while that of the credits granted to the banking sector decreases. Of course, it may occur that the banks make new loans of the money coming from foreign exchange sales, rather than use it to diminish their debt at the central bank. However, since the commercial banks' indebtedness to the central banks is great in a number of West-European countries (especially France), it is probable that they will reduce their debts at the central bank in most cases, although this depends partly on the size of their indebtedness and partly on that of the surplus of the foreign exchange balance. The indebtedness of the German banks to the Bundesbank is rather small and in certain periods capital inflow rose to an unusual extent. Consequently, the German banks loaned out the significant sums they received for the foreign exchange they sold to the Bundesbank, and this resulted in great liquidity. This was, however, an exceptional phenomenon due to exceptional circumstances, while the previous alternative is the general one.

The opposite happens when there is a deficit in the foreign exchange position: banks buy foreign exchange for national currency. To be able to do this, they must obtain national currency from the central bank in the form of a credit, as a result of which their indebtedness towards the central bank grows. Thus, the central bank's foreign exchange reserve decreases, while lending to the banking sector increases. We must add that the money borrowed to make foreign exchange purchases may come not only from the central bank, but also from the banks' clients, which means that the total amount of bank deposits, and hence the volume of credits the banks can grant (the basis of which is formed by the deposits), will decrease. And this brings us to the examination of the behaviour of the economic units, since, in the final analysis, it depends on them whether they wish to meet their foreign exchange obligations by drawing from their own deposits or by drawing credits from their banks.

As for the money-stock and indebtedness of economic units (companies and private individuals), the effects of changes in the foreign exchange situation are more complicated, because a lot of psychological factors play a part as well (which, of course, have their economic basis). In the case of a foreign exchange position with a positive trend the effect can be different depending on whether the propensity to save or to accumulate is strong or weak. If it is weak, the inflow of foreign currency will tend to exert an influence towards the repayment of credits either directly (so that the exporter sells the foreign exchange that he obtained to his bank, thus repaying the drawn credit), or indirectly, as a consequence of the rapid increase of liquidity throughout the economy. If, however, the inclination to accumulate or to refill money holdings is strong, the countervalue of inflown foreign exchange will only slow the growth rate of borrowing but will not lead to repayment, since it will be used partly or in full for accumulation.

This tendency to accumulate is by no means an indifferent matter to the monetary authorities, since the higher the liquidity of economic units is, the less sensitive they are to the restrictive measures that might be introduced later.

The passive trend of the foreign exchange position, however, increases by all means the needs of the economic units for money and credit. It is true that the propensity to accumulate hardly shows up under such circumstances, especially since—apart from other reasons for non-confidence—there is need for other complementary means of financing to replace the outflowing money.

*

Before turning to examine the practical conclusions drawn by the central banks from the above statements—which are far from precise and final, as we have seen—concerning their credit policy measures, we have to make one general and some specific remarks. The objective of the general remark is to define and circumscribe the essence of this chapter, primarily in a negative sense. We do not intend to discuss which of the following means are the most effective to ensure the stability of a currency or to protect against the harmful effects of uncovered international money flows endangering this stability: fiscal or tax policy, price or income policy, perhaps purchasing power policy, maybe issuing or credit policy. It is not our task here to state how these should be applied so that they will not cancel each other's effect. We only wish to point out that uncovered money flows rightly disquiet the central banks, the guardians of currency stability, and they tried to employ a domestic credit policy to limit these money flows and to influence through credit the quantity, pace and direction of these money movements.

It is obvious that in the central banks' arsenal, credit policy plays the primary role, since the other measures mentioned as belonging to various other fields of economic policy are under the state's sphere of authority and not that of the central bank. Central banks seek to influence money flows by credit policy measures in two respects: to prevent money outflow in case the foreign exchange position has a negative tendency, on the one hand, and, on the other, also in the opposite case, when they want to prevent too great a money inflow due to an active trend in the foreign exchange position (imported inflation). The problem to be discussed later is what kind of credit policy measures are adopted by central banks, that is, what credit policy do they follow in these two cases.

Let us first make some preliminary remarks on the basis of the preivously mentioned data collected by the Banque de France, touching upon the central bank's credit policy possibilities. The first remark is that according to the figures the abundance of money and credit seems much more dependent on the factors appearing on the side of demand than on those of supply. If this is really so, the regulation of the *credit volume*, as a means of credit policy, loses some of its importance, and the regulation of the interest level and business activity gains relatively greater emphasis, since demand is obviously influenced by the mutual effect of these two factors. The experiences of the Banque de France, however, contradict this statement. In France, quantitative credit restrictions were in force from time to time, while at other times restrictions of the interest level were used as a means, mainly through non-interest bearing deposits that the banks had to place at the central bank. According to the information of the Banque de France, setting a ceiling on the credit volume was the only really effective measure, while the others had only a very relative effect. The resolution of the contradiction could probably be found in the policy on business cycles, since quantitative credit restrictions were lifted just because they put a brake on the business upturn. Inflation itself increases demand for credit, since in the periods of depreciation of money *indebtedness is a good bargain* even under high interest rate conditions. Thus, in inflationary periods the raising of the interest level hardly affects the demand for credit.

The second remark to be made here is that despite assuming compensation among the counter-items of money issuing, it is not indifferent on what basis the emission takes place, namely, whether the central bank issues money against inflow foreign exchange or against assets in national currency, i.e., against domestic lending. As a matter of fact, with foreign exchange the central bank's money emission goes into effect automatically; however, concerning the quantity and conditions of lending to the economy, the central bank can put its views into practice within the framework of its credit policy. A senior banker from the French central bank expressed this somewhat paradoxically, saying: "If we are forced to make a choice, *domestic* inflation seems to be more tolerable than the imported one, since we can, at least slightly, control and influence the former." The relative weight of issuing against foreign exchange shows, by the way, a decreasing tendency, because in developed capitalist countries the volume of monetary and quasi-monetary emissions and the credit demands on the economy and the Treasury grow equally faster than net foreign claims. This statement is valid, however, only for periods of normal development. In crisis periods massive money inflows may become a primary source of issuing.

For this reason and also because these huge money inflows threw a light on the dangers of imported inflation, it seems necessary to examine the notion itself in detail, all the more as it has already been mentioned several times. According to the classical definition, inflation is a phenomenon or situation when the state of equilibrium between supply and demand tips in favour of demand, when the growth of purchasing power is not met by a matching quantity of goods. Inflation may emerge either from the demand side or from that of production costs, and then it either spreads through the whole economy, or may temporarily appear only in certain sectors. From our viewpoint, there is no need to go beyond this definition—which might be refined in many respects—and it is sufficient to refer to the fact that an excessive (disproportionate) growth of purchasing power leads to inflation. It is equally indifferent whether the changes in demand depend directly on the size of emissions or on the incomes and propensity to accumulate on the part of the economic units. It is obvious that if a country's GNP amounts to 100 billion/annum and the purchasing power is 110 billion, the prices—unless their maximum is set—will increase by 10 percent. Thus, imported inflation means an excessive growth of purchasing power originating from external sources, and as such it comes from the side of demand.

The unhealthy growth of demand influenced from abroad may be direct or indirect. It is direct if it emerges as a consequence of foreign trade impulses, i.e., purchases of great volume at high prices from foreign countries where inflation is already prevailing; it is indirect if through uncovered money flows quite apart from purchases, foreign exchange in quantities above a desirable level flows into the country. These inflown foreign exchange quantities are bought by the central bank against national currency, and in turn the issued domestic money increases purchasing power, and hence—directly or indirectly—(through incomes) the demand.

It logically follows that this indirect form of imported inflation as a consequence of international capital flows—and, owing to its volume, this is the most important and most dangerous form of imported inflation—originates from the mechanism of the international monetary system, and is a function of it. If the central banks were not forced to buy the inflowing foreign exchange, there would not occur any automatic domestic issuing of money. In this respect it is indifferent whether the foreign exchange purchase is done by legal obligation (in case of fixed parities or that of currencies tied to each other) or—in the absence of an intervention obligation—for other, obviously serious reasons. The supporters of pure floating often cite this argument to justify their standpoint. However, as it has been pointed out repeatedly, pure floating is very rare in practice; at most what may happen is that when the inflow of a currency to the central bank reaches an unbearable extent, the bank may temporarily suspend the intervention, i.e., the purchase.

The danger of imported inflation is fairly limited under normal circumstances. This is partly because the size of money flows is substantially smaller, and partly because inflation itself—which causes a strong rise in prices—harms the country's export competitiveness, worsening the trade balance and, through it, the balance of payments, thus leading to an outflow of foreign exchange as a result of wich there is a backflow of the national currency to the central bank, i.e., money withdrawal. However, during crisis periods, which themselves are the result of the international monetary system, these regulating mechanisms cannot assert themselves appropriately.

The question whether the counter-item of issue is lending to the economy or lending to the Treasury is not at all besides the point. The latter is, in fact, fairly insensitive concerning the interest level. If the budget bill is passed, and the respective decisions taken, the Treasury will make use of the credit possibilities regardless of cost. Thus, the central bank does not have the same credit policy means at its disposal towards the Treasury as it does towards companies and individuals, the latter two being interest-sensitive. As it has already been mentioned, interest-sensitivity declines in proportion to climbing inflation. We have pointed out above that money issuing against foreign currencies—if they are presented at the central bank—is automatic. We have to add that the commercial banks themselves decide on the use or eventual placing of home currency flowing to them as a consequence of the central bank's purchases of inflowing foreign exchange, hence also in respect of the increase of the credit volume. In this way, imported inflation decreases the effectiveness of the credit policy measures through both a decrease in the interest-sensitivity of the economic units and this possibility of free decision on the part of the banks. We have also seen that during troubled periods, measures to prevent money outflow are hardly effective. We see that the central bank is almost powerless regarding the Treasury, partly because the Treasury is hardly sensitive to the interest level and partly because of the central bank's position. The only field where central credit policy may exert its full efficacy is the field of money issue against credit to the economy. This is why the credit policy cannot be the only means of economic policy and it bears fruit only if it is complemented or joined by adequate budgetary and taxation policies.

Let us add here that according to another theory the important interconnection is not to be looked for between liquidity (monetary and quasi-monetary assets together), but is to be found in the relationship between the balance of payments and the growth rate of the quantity of money only. A brief summary of this concept is as follows: Periodically (yearly) issued money either remains actual money or becomes a deposit. The issue may be effected either against inflown foreign exchange, or against lending in domestic currency. Thus on the active side of the issuing balance, the total annual variations of foreign exchange and credits must be equal to the total variations of banknotes and deposits on the passive side. The counterpart of banknotes are the foreign exchange and credits financed by the central bank, while that of the deposits are loans financed by the commercial banks. The deposits can be converted into money at any time. This happens when the central bank refinances the commercial banks. If foreign exchange is flowing to the central bank the growth rate of banknotes accelerates; if there is an outflow, it slows down. It is true that the lack of foreign exchange may be substituted by the central bank's increasing refinancing of commercial banks, but usually this only occurs on a small scale, because just when the balance of payments shows a deficit, the central bank, in order to avoid inflationary effects, tries to reduce the refinancing of commercial banks, and it is inclined to be generous in this respect when the foreign exchange situation is favourable. In this way the changes in the balance of payments have a direct influence on the growth rate of the quantity of banknotes.

Professor Chaineau, an expert on theoretical problems of the balance of payments, has presented data supporting the above concept. He counterposted for the period of the 12 years preceding the franc-crisis of 1968 the not balance of inflown and outflown currencies to and from the French banking system, on the one hand, and the growth rate expressed in a percentage of the quantity of money in circulation, on the other.

It can be stated on the basis of his figures that there is a certain correlation between the two factors mentioned, and also that this relationship is not unconditional. When the balance of payments shows a surplus, the growth rate of the quantity of money becomes faster, and a balance-of-payments deficit slows the growth of the quantity of money to a less degree than the surplus accelerates it. The reason for this is obviously that the other two sources of money issue—lending to the Treasury and to the economic units—compensate to a certain extent the drop in issuance against foreign exchange. The extent of this compensation depends on the central bank's credit policy.

The scope of this study does not include a critical examination of the above-presented theory on the interconnections between the amount of money in circulation and the balance of payments. For our purposes it is sufficient to state that the interconnection to be proved is not automatic, even if it is direct, since at least to a certain extent the refinancing, i.e., the credit policy of the central bank plays a role in it. Hence, we are again back at the concrete problems of credit policy applied in connection with the changes in the equilibrium of the balance of payments.

Experience shows that, in connection with the changes in the tendencies of the balance of payments, in the foreign exchange position, the central banks generally tend to adopt restrictive credit policy measures almost regardless of these tendencies. This is natural when the trend is negative, since a money outflow is usually a sign and consequence of inflationary pressures and both the prevention of price rises and the improvement of the foreign exchange situation justify a restrictive credit policy. But the propensity to carry out such a policy is also manifested if the currency inflow is very strong. It is perhaps so because the interconnection mentioned above is not considered absolute; the central banks are afraid of the strong growth of liquidity, of imported inflation and, therefore, they try to counteract them through credits, i.e., in an artificial way.

The acceptance as fact of the reviewed phenomena of mutual effects does not at all mean that the credit policy to be followed can be derived from it in a logical way. From the premise of the real existence of this interdependence, there may follow actually two equally logical consequences in diametrical opposition, between which there can be almost innumerable intermediate standpoints. The two extreme conclusions are fatalism and total severity. True, if the foreign exchange position worsens, it is no wonder that the credit volume increases, since the economy's need for money must be satisfied. Thus, there is no use interfering, and credits should be allowed to occupy the place of foreign exchange as a counterpart of liquidity. This is the fatalist standpoint.

But the standpoint of total severity also can be logically justified: as in certain periods economic units need a given amount of liquidity, the volume of liquidity is necessarily given, so the channels of credit must be closed as that would prevent the outflow of money. This reasoning justifies a very severe credit policy.

Just because of the wide scale of logical possibilities, the question must be raised as to the aim of credit policy, its possibilities, political and social limits. It is not easy to determine the goals of credit policy. Roughly, we may say that these goals are of two types: of a monetary and of a general economic character. The monetary objectives are fundamentally directed at maintaining the balance-of-payments equilibrium and the possible stability of the price level. These aims may be attained or approached through interventions of a restrictive character.

Economic goals—and social aims are a part of them, too—mean the maintenance of prosperity, of economic growth and a favourable level of employment. These goals are more likely to be attained through a flexible and liberal credit policy.

Let us see how central banks reconcile in practice the requirements and opposite means coming from the two goals, and what kind of an actual credit policy they pursue. Neither of the two, logically equally possible extreme standpoints reviewed above is usually adapted by the central banks; they carry out neither a fully liberal, nor a socially and economically unbearable, absolutely restrictive credit policy. Their credit policy is more pragmatic and empirical than dogmatic.

If the balance of payments shows a surplus, the central bank may, in principle, introduce a more permissive credit policy, it may allow a more ample and cheaper credit supply, thereby stimulating the development of the economy as the national currency requires no defence, unless against revaluation endangering the country's export-competitiveness. Nevertheless, wishing to avoid imported inflation, the central bank usually does not (or only slightly) apply looser measures and keeps the interest relatively high, which does not promote the restoration of equilibrium but may lead to further money inflows. Central banks quite often try to counterbalance short-term money inflows by measures promoting long-term foreign placements—as has been done by the Bundesbank for a long time. In the final analysis, this does not lead to the restoration of equilibrium either. The conclusion to be drawn is that the central bank's credit policy reacts only slowly and very cautiously to the favourable development of the foreign exchange position.

If the foreign exchange position is unfavourable, the central bank's credit policy is again a result of compromise. The compromise is established between the monetary and the economic targets. Certainly, the greater the danger from the monetary side and the lower the central bank reserves, the more severe is their credit policy, because in such periods its measures are employed primarily to attain monetary goals. At that time the central bank keeps the interest level high to promote the inflow of money and to cut down on borrowing by the economic units. In order to reach the latter goal, quantitative credit regulations are applied periodically. These can only be successful if adequate measures tending towards severeness are adopted in the other economic policy fields, too, especially in the budgetary and tax policies, and in the wages and incomes policy.

In this context let us note in parentheses that the covering of budget deficits means certain burden to the money market. In the final analysis, the bigger the deficit to be financed from the money market is, the smaller the amount that the economic units can get in the form of credits, and thus the interest level is higher. This is no longer true if the deficit is covered by sources independent of the market. This was the case in the second half of 1971 in the United States when the European and Japanese central banks, as a consequence of the well-known events, could not otherwise use the dollars flown to them, but were compelled to buy US Treasury bills (more than 25 billion dollars' worth), which, covering the bulk of the record budget deficit, led to a drop in the US domestic money market's interest level.

By the beginning of the 1980's the United States government budget deficit had increased to such an extent that it could be financed only at very high money market interests. This was accompanied by profound consequences in terms of both the domestic US economy and the international monetary situation. The high US interest levels attracted a major influx of money and, raising Eurodollar interests, it led to other currencies being exchanged for US dollars on a vast scale, which was further stimulated by growing international tensions with people looking for shelters for their money. The situation led to a strengthening of the dollar's exchange rate. The economic problems posited by an overvalued dollar for the other participants in the international monetary system are well known.

To return to our train of thought, we must state that the fundamental problem of every credit policy is to know just how far it is possible to go in severity in order to defend monetary interests, without having the stabilization policy bring an end to prosperity, disrupt the development of the country's economic growth, worsen the employment situation, i.e., bring on unemployment. It is impossible to resolve this contradiction in principle and very difficult in practice. It cannot be attempted otherwise than through cautious, pragmatic measures complementing each other, the success of which is always relative, never immediate and can only be real if it is lasting.

The conclusion that can be drawn from what has been said above about the credit policy of the developed capitalist countries is a rather disappointing one. Although the problem has been treated in a simplified manner and several factors (like, e.g., the problem of prices, which otherwise is of primary importance from the aspect of the examined topic) have been consciously neglected, it can be nevertheless stated that the supposition of regular interrelations between the balance of payments or foreign exchange position and the domestic credit or the quantity of money also fails to make it possible to carry out a credit policy, in fact not even an economic policy, which would be able to save the individual countries' economy from dangers stemming from uncovered international money flows. The reason for that lies partly in the mechanism of the international monetary system and partly, perhaps mostly, in the frequently occurring situation in which monetary targets and the maintenance of prosperity get into a seemingly irresolvable contradiction. Yet, in one form or another, at one time or another, all developed capitalist countries have to face that dilemma, because the money flows in question originate from objective factors.

Chapter VI

Summary and Conclusions

The previous chapters reviewed the nature, phenomena, causes and effects of international money and capital flows descriptively more from a practical aspect. The aim of this chapter is to summarize the essence of the other chapters in order to draw some conclusions. It would be hard to accomplish this task without giving a certain outline of principles and a theoretical underpinning to this summary. This shall be our endeavour in the following, while not pretending to form any model.

Perhaps the best way to approach the question is to group all that we are going to say around one concept—the balance of payments—since, as it is clear from the descriptive part of our study, international money and capital flows are realized, can be measured and exert their influence in this area. Let us examine the role of the balance of payments first in a homogeneous monetary space where there are no banks, then let us draw the existence of the banking system into our examination, and finally, coming closer to reality, let us carry out our examination in the case of several monetary spaces having several individual banking systems.

The notion of the balance of payments is, in fact, very simple. Each economic unit has its own balance of payments expressing the balance of its incomes and expenditures. If we add up the expenditures and the incomes of n economic units, we get the *total* balance of payments of these economic units, just as if we had totalized of these their individual balances. From this, if the economic units acting in the same monetary space are in a trading relationship and there is no bank, and hence no issuance—as a consequence of which mutual payments can be settled only out of the money stock previously hoarded—the following conclusions can be drawn:

1. In a closed circle, the sum of expenditures must be equal to the sum of incomes, cince the incomes of the participants can come only from the expenditures of other participants.

2. If we assume that there are no banks, *global* hoarding cannot be assumed either. The hoarding by individual economic units, the global surplus of their balance of payments equal the diminution of the hoarded stock, the global deficit of the balance of payments of other economic units. This means that the payment turnover among the economic units is settled exclusively in previously created money.

3. This zero balance of global hoarding is independent of the intentions of the economic units. What can be changed by their will is the volume of the transactions. If an economic unit intends to restore its balance-of-payments equilibrium (does not want to decrease its money stock further), it has to decrease its expenditures, the total volume of its purchases.

These statements are valid not only for the individual economic units and their totality but, within it, also for groups of economic units. This means that the result of our examination can also be transposed to the international level. As there are economic units needing financing while others have surplusses and are able to finance, so there are also deficit-burdened countries needing financing and countries with surplusses able to provide that financing. Thus, if the countries—like the economic units in our example above—could settle the deficit of their payments balance only from the gold and foreign exchange stock previously hoarded (in our example, the starting point was the assumption of the nonexistence of any banks and that of monetary issue) it would have to entail the decrease in foreign transactions, as these stocks are limited and therefore have to be treated carefully. Under such circumstances, the balance of payments could, of course, be brought into equilibrium until the mentioned stocks—the reserves—last.

A more permanent deficit is made possible only by one factor—the credit—i.e., the monetary issue taking place for this reason. In order to be able to approach the real situation, we must include this factor in our example, with the aid of which the decrease in world-trade turnover can be avoided. Let us see how this factor asserts itself first of all in a closed economic space, within an imagined country with no contacts abroad.

Economic units within a country (enterprises and households) can be divided into two categories: the ones which need financing and the ones which are able to provide it. Roughly, one may say that enterprises are globally in the need category, and households have the surplus. These two groups are linked by the banks so that from and on the basis of the deposits placed by the possessors of surplus they execute monetary issuance in favour of the economic units needing financing, in the form of lending to the latter group. Thus, the spending possibilities of the economic units needing financing (i.e., with payments balances in the red) are not limited up to the total of their incomes and the diminution of their stocks, but they grow by the amount of the monetary issue in their favour, i.e., by the amount of bank credit granted to them. Issuing makes it also possible that individual economic units should be able to satisfy their hoarding intentions. The amount of global hoarding is in this case actually equal to that of the global diminution of the money stock plus the monetary issuance.

If we project what has been said about the balance of payments in general to an international scale, to the relationship between countries, then the balance of payments of a given country will show the balance of foreign trade and foreign financial transactions of that country's every economic unit, while domestic transactions will be disregarded. If the balance of payments is positive, then this balance expresses the net claims against foreign banks, while if it is negative, it expresses the net liabilities of domestic banks towards foreign ones. Thus, the balance of payments has an influence on the country's domestic liquidity, too, because the owners of foreign monetary claims—either because of regulations or of their own free will (in the latter case less automatically) —convert them into national currency in a way that they cede them to the banks which will carry out a money issue against these claims in favour of the economic units which have ceded them. Hence the interconnection between domestic and external liquidity.

But the domestic and the external monetary position can never be the same. However big the surplus of a country's balance of payments may be, it can never cover the financing needs of the economy. These needs always exceed those possibilities of issuance which come from the external monetary position of the country, and which otherwise, in case of a deficit in the balance of payments, may turn negative as the national currency paid out for the purchased foreign exchange and going to the central bank will be withdrawn. Despite all these, external liquidity is an essential factor of the domestic one, and makes it easier to meet the domestic requirements of liquidity. The nature of these relations has been dealt with in detail in the previous chapter, and there is no need to return to the question.

If we examine the settlement of international payments more closely, we may draw the conclusion that the payments of a client of a domestic bank transferred to a client of a foreign bank has the result that finally the domestic bank becomes the debtor of the foreign one. If the country's balance of payments shows a deficit, the banking system of the country becomes net indebted to foreign banks, and the negative balance expresses the size of this indebtedness. Thus, *mutatis mutandis*, the situation occurs which has been outlined with the assumption of a closed economic space and the non-existence of banks.

What is the solution to this situation? The first and the simplest way is to settle the obligation by transferring gold or foreign exchange. As a result of this move the external liquidity of the debtor country's banking system will decrease; in order to avoid this tendency, the given country will be forced to lead a deflationary policy, to reduce the turnover with her foreign partners in order to save her gold and foreign exchange reserver. From this aspect, the hidden purpose behind the creation of the SDR was that, increasing the transferable gold and currency stocks by the IMF paper gold, the countries with deficits would be less compelled to narrow their external economic relations in order to save their reserves.

Another possible way to solve the problem is if a creditor country agrees not to recover its claim, i.e., not to present its claim to the debtor to be settled. This solution avoids the „narrowing" effect reviewed in the previous paragraph, since in this case the debtor country's reserves do not decrease, and neither does its external liquidity. The creditor country always monetizes its excess in foreign exchange, i.e., issues national currency against them, but the debtor country is not obliged under such circumstances to demonetize its deficit. This is the situation in the case of the balance of payments of the United States. The developed capitalist countries have exempted the United States from having to settle its deficit of balance of payments because of the dollar's key currency nature and its role in international payments. Thus was the Eurodollar born. The other Eurocurrencies also originate from the fact that foreign banks do not collect their claims in the given currency—although they could do so in contrast to the Eurodollars—but keep them because they are in use on the international money markets. The Eurocurrencies are the subject of international turnover and most of them never get back to the issuing central bank for conversion, i.e., for demonetization. Their existence, coming from non-conversion, greatly promotes the growth of international liquidity. Thus, in fact, the situation was solved through money issuance.

A further solution is the swap, which has already been discussed. Here we have to remark only that this operation leads to a temporary issuing of the creditor's currency. The issuance is temporary because the repayment abolishes it a few months later. If the quantity of swaps permanently grows and after the repayment of old swaps new ones of greater amounts are granted, this temporariness can, of course, be interpreted in a fairly broad sense.

Finally, the situation can also be solved so that the debtor country's banking system borrows the lost money from the creditor country's banking system or other economic units if those have held it. This is the case when the outflown capital is directed back within the framework of inter-central-bank cooperation (recycling) and also when US banks borrow Eurodollars.

*

The slightly schematic above summary and the subject of this study itself need some final commentary, even if we expose ourselves to the danger of repetition. First of all, perhaps, it should be stressed that the existence and growth of the Euromarket and the ever increasing volume of swap deals have greatly broadened international liquidity. The international monetary market coming into being this way has led in practice to the supremacy of one national currency—the dollar—and of one banking system—that of the United States. The Federal Reserve System has started to take the same attitude towards the banks playing an active role on the international money market as that taken by the central bank within the national banking system. This fact has unequivocally raised the question of trust or mistrust in the dollar.

Actually, the relative stability of the international capitalist monetary system is, or more exactly was, based on the fact that from the banks of the participating countries there was as much of a permanent demand for the dollar as there is in the national banking system for the money issued by the central bank. And this is, in the final analysis, a question of trust. Where are the limits to this trust, what are the causes leading to its relative weakening, what reforms does the international monetary system need in order to base its stability not only on this single factor, are all questions which essentially do belong to the subject of our study, but since they do only indirectly, we will not deal with these aspects.

Nevertheless, we must remark that the development of the Euromarkets and the increasing volume of international money flows have deeply changed the "classical" face of the capitalist monetary system, and this change through the interrelations has exerted a far-reaching influence on the whole of the economy of all of the participating countries, and even on the uncertain monetary situation which has developed as a consequence of these factors.

According to the classical theory, the central bank issued money either against gold or against credit lent to the economy or to the Treasury. The quantity of gold was given and the credit could, to a certain extent, be regulated by the central bank. The general acceptance of the gold-exchange standard meant that the central bank was obliged to issue money also against a third source, namely against foreign exchange, i.e., against a currency issued by a foreign country in an arbitrary amount. The gold-exchange standard is the factor which provided the possibility that a country's issuing policy should become dependent on the issuing policy of other foreign countries—in reality, of the economically and politically most powerful one. This statement is even more valid for the circumstances of the *de facto* dollar standard emerging after the breakdown of the Bretton Woods system. The accomplishment of the thus given possibility occurred, however, as a consequence of the permanently growing volume of international money flows and that of the importance of Eurocurrency markets. Here indeed quantity has turned into quality, and has changed the substance of the international monetary system.

Until the recent past, money issuing has been an element or—one can say—one of the criteria of national sovereignty. Although the royal right to mint has undergone a change, and the central bank has become the executive organ of national sovereignty in this field, and although this right has later become significantly decentralized in favour of the other participants of the country's banking system, yet, money issuance has been, up to very recently, under state control through the central bank. The phenomena examined in our study have led to the situation whereby this right has *de facto* slipped out of the control of the states participating in the international monetary system. It is hard to tell in whose favour, although some signs point to the fact that directly or indirectly it favours the United States. The fact that monetary issuance needs control and regulation can hardly be debated. It is questionable, however, whether the United States will be able to exercise this function in the given situation. If the answer is positive, it means US supremacy over the countries participating in the international monetary system. If it is negative—because the system will develop in a way which eliminates the possibilities of central control—the consequences are unforeseeable, since no otherwise desirable effective international control can be expected, due to the contradiction of interests among the participating countries. So the individual countries will be compelled to bring about restrictive measures, which, in turn, will limit the freedom of the flow of goods and capital that had been meant to be secured at Bretton Woods.

The alternatives we seem to have allow for pessimism, since they can be summed up as follows: US supremacy or protectionism. Efforts to reform the international monetary system, of course, aim to solve this dilemma. It is another question how far these endeavours can be successful considering the balance of forces within the IMF where the United States plays the dominant role. Anyway, the resolutions adopted in Jamaica postponed the execution of the reform to the far future, to a moment "when the stability of the general economic situation will be restored, and as a consequence of this, such a general arrangement will become possible which might be acceptable both to the countries with balance-of-payments deficits and surpluses". The IMF will decide when this will take place. Until then, the present chaotic situation remains in force, but now with the IMF's confirmation.

It is unscholarly and risky to enter into predictions, still, it seems proper to put forward some ideas as to what the international monetary system to replace Bretton Woods should be like.

Obviously, the composition of its board and its appropriate sphere of authority as well as an inherent automatism limiting the necessity of *ad hoc* measures should ensure its functioning. Also it should secure the desirable freedom as well as the necessary control of goods and money flows. It ought to be such that the supremacy of one national currency—the dollar—should not come into being and none of the participant countries should enjoy disproportionate advantages to the detriment of others. Under the given circumstances, however, one must be aware of the fact that the international monetary system that will be finally born will be far from being in conformity to this ideal, but a compromise, based on the balance of forces at the time of the reform's realization, will decide on the extent to which it will be approximated.

The new international monetary system could be really appropriate only if it were truly international, that is, if it were formed with the participation of all the countries of the world. Until important countries are missing from it, the system, *ipso facto*, remains imperfect.

Still, it is desirable to take a look at the essence of the reform decided at the IMF conference in Jamaica, although it cannot be considered final as it was postponed indefinitely. The parities serving as a basis for a general exchange rate system are planned to be stable but adjustable. The permissible fluctuation from the average rate (parity) can be ±4.5 percent. Every country must take care that the spot rate of its own currency against the currencies of the other member countries should remain within this limit on the domestic foreign exchange market. Parities can be expressed in SDRs or another "denominator", but not in gold or in the currency of other member countries. In order to maintain balance-of-payments equilibrium, the member countries may, with IMF approval, change the parity of their own currency, may suspend it, i.e., may let it float, and later they may establish a new parity with the help of another denominator. The IMF has a certain right to control the decisions of member countries in these questions.

This is what was essentially stated—even if in a circumscribed and loosely composed form—in the amendment of the chart, decided in principle in Jamaica. If we compare these heavily modified ideas with the Bretton Woods monetary system, with those of its stipulations which in practice led to the supremacy of the United States, undoubtedly, we can notice a certain progress. The Bretton Woods monetary system ensured two main privileges for the United States. The first came from the gold-exchange standard, or more exactly, from the dollar's role as a key currency, as a consequence of which the USA could cover its balance-of-payments deficits by issuing dollars to an arbitrary degree. This privilege has ceased to exist, since a national currency—including the dollar—can no longer be the basis of a parity and thus the dollar's role as a key currency is being dropped. The other privilege consisted of the fact that the Federal Reserve System was not obliged to intervene in favour of the dollar. This is no longer the case, since the obligation to intervene in favour of one's own currency holds each member country according to the amendment of the chart. The counter-item of this privilege, the obligation to convert into gold, has also ended, of course, since gold was eliminated from the international monetary system.

All these mean a step forward only in respect of the elimination of negative aspects, but they hardly bring about any positive solution. The efforts of the IMF tend obviously towards a substitution of SDRs for gold, so that SDRs should play the role of the "main denominator" in determining parities and that of the "principal reserve asset". This will most probably lead to the issuing of further and significant amounts of SDR. And the SDR's specific nature is to be "easily creatable", since according to the decision of the IMF they can be issued and allocated in any amounts and at any time among the participant member countries. This, however, makes the question of the regulation of international liquidity dependent on the power relationships within the IMF. It is true, that nowadays, in the time of the *de facto* dollar standard, such questions are decided actually within the USA's sphere of influence.

And if the power relationships within the IMF do not change, the situation concerning the USA's dominance will remain essentially the same in the future, even if the changeover to the SDR standard does happen.

The concept concerning the reform of the capitalist international monetary system embodied in the resolutions in Jamaica leave open several important problems. It would be superfluous to enumerate all of them here. For our purposes it is enough to point out that in respect of the control of international money flows, just like in that of the regulation of Eurocredit markets, the resolutions do not even make a reference, although we have seen their importance in view of monetary stability.

No matter how the world economy will develop, whenever and under what conditions the reform of the international monetary system will be attained, the economic relations among the individual countries will be carried out invariably through the international money flows, and thus problems concerning these will never cease being with us.

Bibliography

Aftalion, Albert: *Monnaie, prix et change*, Paris, Sirey, 1940, p. 565.

Алмазова, О.—Миронов, И.: "Различные оцсики дефицита платэзного баланса США" (Evaluation of the US balance of payments deficit), BIKI, 1971, April 27, No. 2, p. 8.

Аникин, А.: "Валютный кризис капитализма: причины и последэтвия" (The currency crisis of capitalism: its causes and consequences), *Коммунист*, 1971 (July), No. 10, pp. 91-102.

Bácskai, Tamás: "A tőkés nemzetközi pénzügyi rendszer strukturális zavarai" (Structural disorders in the international capitalist monetary system), *Pénzügyi Szemle*, 1969, No. 3, pp. 190-198.

Bácskai, Tamás: "A tőkés világ pénzügyi rendszerének aktuális problémái" (Current problems of the capitalist monetary system), *Közgazdasági Szemle*, 1971, No. 7-8, pp. 868-879.

Banque de France: *Colloque d'information sur les problèmes internes de liquidité*, Paris, Banque de France, 1966, p. 115.

Bakó, Ede: "A fejlett nyugati országok valutaárfolyam-rendszerének néhány problémája és perspektívája" (Some problems and prospects of the currency exchange system of the developed Western countries), *Pénzügyi Szemle*, 1970, No. 5, pp. 432-440.

Bánfi, Tamás: "A valutaárfolyam problémája a tőkés monetáris rendszerben" (The problems of the exchange rate of currencies in the capitalist monetary system), *Pénzügyi Szemle*, 1970, No. 6, pp. 510-517.

Barrère, Alain: *Politique financière*, Paris, Dalloz, 1958, p. 595.

Becsky, György: "A magántőkemozgások liberalizálásának útja és problémái Nyugat-Európában a II. világháború után" (Progress and problems of the liberalization of private capital flows in Western Europe after the Second World War), *Közgazdasági Szemle*, 1969, No. 2, pp. 216-224.

Becsky, György: "A hosszú lejáratú nemzetközi magántőkemozgások az európai OECD országokban, 1960-1965" (Long-term international private capital flows in the European OECD countries, 1960-1965), *Közgazdasági Szemle*, 1969, No. 7-8, pp. 955-969.

Berger, Pierre: *Le marché monétaire et le marché des changes*, Paris, Les Cours de Droit, 1957, p. 259.

Berger, Pierre: *La monnaie et ses mécanismes*, Paris, P.U.F., 1966, p. 125.

Besse, Pierre: *Institutions et mécanismes monétaires,* Paris, Les Cours de Droit, 1955; 1968, p. 401.

Biacabe, Pierre: *Analyses contemporaines de l'inflation*, Paris, Sirey, 1962, p. 359.

Bloomfeld, Arthur L.: "Mouvements de capitaux et crises monétaires", *Economie Appliquée*, Geneva, 1970, No. 4.

Bourcier de Carbone, Luc: *Analyse économique*, Vol. II, *La monnaie et le crédit*, Paris, Montchrestien, 1970, p. 427.

Brochier, Hubert—Tabatoni, Pierre: *Economie financière*, Paris, P.U.F., 1959, p. 695.

Caubque, Pierre: *La masse monétaire*, Paris, Editions de l'Epargne, 1960, p. 63.

Chaineau, André: *Mécanismes et politique monétaires*, Paris, P.U.F., 1968, p. 218.

Colin de Verdière, Gérard: *Conjoncture et monnaie*, Paris, Sirey, 1960, p. 127.

Доронин, И. Г.: "Об обострении кризиса капиталистической валютной системи" (The sharpening crisis of the capitalist currency system), BIKI, 1971, June 1, No. 2, p. 9.

Einzig, Paul: *The Euro-dollar System*, London, MacMillan, 1964. p. 164.

Einzig, Paul: *Foreign Exchange Crises*, London, MacMillan, 1970, p. 204.

Erős, Gyula: "Magyar szemmel a tőkés nemzetközi pénzügyek néhány kérdéséről" (On some problems of international capitalist finance from a Hungarian viewpoint), *Közgazdasági Szemle*, 1970, No 7-8, pp. 945-959.

Esteva, Pierre: *Les monnaies de réserve et la liquidité internationale*, Paris, Les Cours de Droit, 1961, p. 27.

Fekete, János: "Napirenden a nemzetközi valutáris rendszer reformja" (The reform of the international currency system is on the agenda), *Népszabadság*, September 1, 1971, p. 10.

Fekete, János: "Tőkés valutaválság = dollárválság" (Capitalist currency crisis = dollar crisis), *Népszabadság*, May 26, 1971, p. 10.

Friedman, Milton: *The Optimum Quantity of Money*, London, MacMillan, 1969.

Friedman, Milton: *Inflation et systèmes monétaires*, Paris, Calmann-Lévy, 1969, p. 310.

Friedman, M.—Heller, W.: *Politique monétaire ou fiscale*, Paris, Mame, 1969, p. 142.

Gyöngyössy, István: "A pénzpiacok és a tőkés nemzetközi pénzrendszer átalakulása" (Transformation of the money markets and the international capitalist monetary system), *Gazdaság*, December 1970, No. 4, pp. 108-117.

Hawtrey, R. G.: *La circulation monétaire et le crédit*, Paris, Sirey, 1935, p. 647.

Heilperin, Michel: *Monnaie, crédit et transfert*, Paris, Sirey, 1932, p. 143.

Hein, John: "Pour comprendre la balance des paiements des Etats Unis", *Banque*, Paris, 1971, Nos 297 and 298.

Jacobsson, Per: *Some Monetary Problems: International and National*, Oxford University Press, 1958, p. 225.

Jacobsson, Per: *International Monetary Problems. 1957-63*, Washington, F.M.I., 1964, p. 368.

James, Emile: *Problèmes monétaires d'aujourd'hui*, Paris, Sirey, 1964, p. 353.
Jasinszky, Pierre: *Régime juridique de la libre circulation des capitaux*, Paris, L.G.D.J., 1967, p. 340.
Keviczky, Lóránd: "Az eurodollár-piac" (The Euro-dollar market), *Külkereskedelem*, 1969, No. 4, pp. 111-112; No. 5, pp. 141-144.
Keviczky, Lóránd: "Merre tart a tőkés nemzetközi valutarendszer?" (Where is the international capitalist currency system heading?), *Külkereskedelem*, 1970, No. 9, pp. 273-275.
Keviczky, Lóránd: "A tőkés valutarendszer újabb megrázkódtatása" (A new crisis of the capitalist currency system), *Külkereskedelem*, 1971, No. 7, pp. 193-196.
Keynes, J. M.: *Théorie générale de l'emploi, de l'intéret et de la monnaie*, Paris, Payot, 1949, p. 407.
Koch, H.: "Etude sur la vitesse de la circulation de la monnaie en France", *Banque*, April 1959, No. 154.
Kövér, Károly: *Miért kerülnek válságba a tőkés valuták?* (Why do Capitalist Currencies Get into Crises?), Budapest, Közgazdasági és Jogi Könyvkiadó, 1971, p. 240.
Kövér, Károly: *A tőkés világ valutarendszere* (The Currency System of the Capitalist World), Budapest, Közgazdasági és Jogi Könyvkiadó, 1967, p. 243.
Lacour, C.: "Mouvements internationaux des capitaux à court terme et taux d'intéret", *Revue de Science Financière*, 1968, No. 3.
Lantos, Imre and Lőrinczné Istvánffy Hajnal: *A nemzetközi valutáris kapcsolatok fejlődésének új tényezői* (New Factors in the Development of International Currency Relations), Budapest, Közgazdasági és Jogi Könyvkiadó, 1974.
Le Bourva, Jacques: *L'inflation française d'après-guerre 1945-1949*, Paris, A. Collin, 1953, p. 381.
"Le mystère des capitaux flottants", *Problèmes Economiques*, No. 1104.
Machlup, Fritz: *International Monetary Economics*, London, G. Allen, 1964, p. 471.

Marchal, Jean: *Monnaie et crédit*, Paris, Cujas, 1970, p. 476.

Майоров, Е.: "Международные валютные проблемы" (International currency problems), *Внешняя торговля*, 1970, No. 6, p. 17-21.

Maison, Maurice: *Travaux du Congrès des Economistes de langue française 1955. Convertibilité et libération des échanges*, Paris, Ed. Montchrestien, 1956, p. 224.

Mayer, Helmut, W.: "Le marché de l'eurodollar et la mobilité internationale des capitaux", *Economie Appliquée*, Geneva, 1970, No. 4.

Mosse, Robert: *Les problèmes monétaires internationaux au tournant des années 1970*, Paris, Payot, 1970, p. 479.

Munier, Bertrand: *Le cambisme et le jeu monétaire international*, Paris, P.U.F., 1970, p. 383.

Nogaro, Bertrand: *La monnaie et les systèmes monétaires*, Paris, L.D.G.J., 1948, p. 295.

OCDE: *Les mécanismes d'ajustement des balances des paiements*, Paris, OCDE, 1966, p. 33.

Ponsard, Cl.: "La théorie quantitative de la monnaie", *Annales*, January 1959, No. 1.

Rapport Wormser—Rapport sur le marché monétaire et les conditions du crédit, Paris, Documentation Française, June 1969, p. 57.

Rist, Charles: *Histoire des doctrines relatives au crédit et à la monnaie depuis John Law jusqu'à nos jours*, Paris, Sirey, 1951, p. 540.

Rueff, Jacques: *La réforme du système monétaire international*. Paris, France-Empire, 1967, p. 190.

Rueff, Jacques: *Le péché monétaire de l'Occident*, Paris, Plon, 1971, p. 282.

Sulyok, Béla: "A tőkés integráció jövője és a nemzetközi valutarendszer" (The prospects of capitalist integration and the international currency system), *Pénzügyi Szemle*, 1970, No. 5, pp. 361-378.

Szigeti, Pál: "A nemzetközi likviditásteremtés új rendszerének néhány elméleti és gyakorlati problémája" (Some theoretical and practical problems of the new system for creating international liquidity), *Gazdaság*, 1970, No. 3.

Смыслов, Д.: "Кризис международного валютного механизма" (Crisis of the international currency system), *Мировая Экономика* 1971, No. 7, pp. 12-28.

Стадниченко, А. И.: *Валютный кризис капитализма*, (Currency crisis in capitalism), Moscow, Международные Отношения, 1970, p. 252.

Triffin, Robert: *L'or et la crise du dollar*, Paris, P.U.F., 1962, p. 203.

Triffin, Robert: *Le système monétaire international*, Paris, 1969, p. 293.

Vinay, Bernard: *Economie monétaire*, Paris, A. Colin, 1970, p. 352.

Weiller, Jean: *La balance des payments*, Paris, P.U.F., 1968, p. 128.

Wiesel, Iván: "Válságban a tőkés valutáris rendszer" (The capitalist currency system in crisis), *Gazdaság*, 1969, No. 1, pp. 93-101.

Wiesel, Iván: "A tőkés országok kamatszínvonalának nemzetközi összehasonlító elemzése" (An international comparative analysis of interest levels in the capitalist countries), *Pénzügyi Szemle*, 1969, No. 7, pp. 548-560.

GPSR Compliance

The European Union's (EU) General Product Safety Regulation (GPSR) is a set of rules that requires consumer products to be safe and our obligations to ensure this.

If you have any concerns about our products, you can contact us on ProductSafety@springernature.com

In case Publisher is established outside the EU, the EU authorized representative is:

Springer Nature Customer Service Center GmbH
Europaplatz 3
69115 Heidelberg, Germany

Batch number: 10830939

Printed by Printforce, the Netherlands